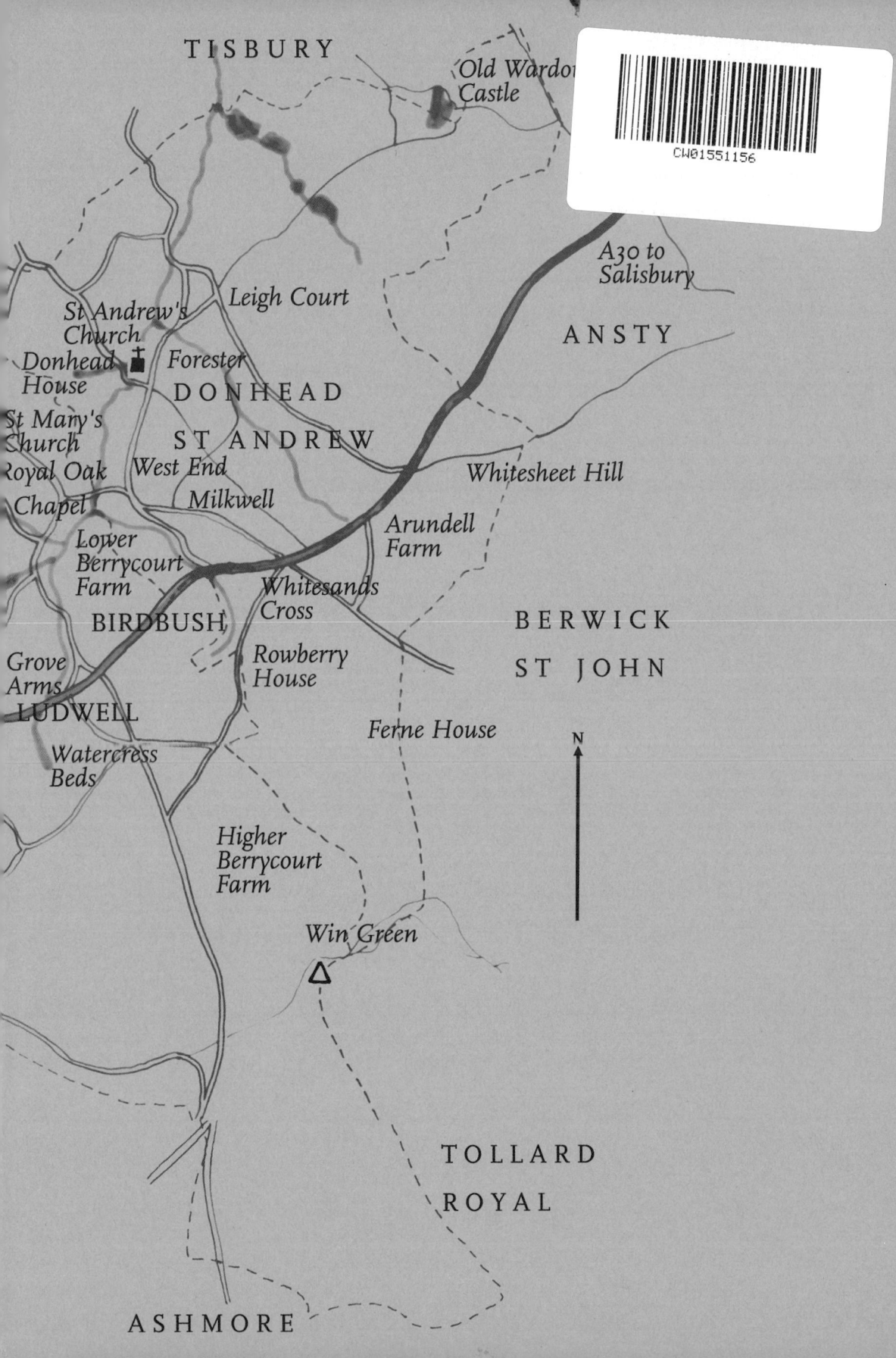

TISBURY

Old Wardour
Castle

A30 to
Salisbury

ANSTY

Leigh Court

St Andrew's
Church
Donhead
House
Forester

DONHEAD

St Mary's
Church

ST ANDREW

Royal Oak
West End

Whitesheet Hill

Chapel
Milkwell

Arundell
Farm

Lower
Berrycourt
Farm

Whitesands
Cross

BIRDBUSH

BERWICK

Grove
Arms

Rowberry
House

ST JOHN

LUDWELL

Ferne House

Watercress
Beds

N

Higher
Berrycourt
Farm

Win Green

TOLLARD

ROYAL

ASHMORE

THE DONHEADS ~ PAST AND PRESENT

The Donheads
past & present

BY

MICHAEL COWARD
DAVID M^CLEAN
REX SAWYER
CHRISTINE SPEAK

First published in the United Kingdom in 2007 by The Hobnob Press, PO Box 1838, East Knoyle, Salisbury SP3 6FA, with the Donhead St Mary Village Hall Committee.

British Library Cataloguing in Publication Data
A catalogue record for this book is available from the British Library.

Acknowledgements
The authors and publisher are grateful for the help received from Anna McDowell, Mike Montgomery and members of the Donhead St Mary Village Hall Committee.

ISBN 978-0-946418-64-0

Typeset in 11/15 pt Scala
Typesetting and origination by John Chandler
Printed in Great Britain by Salisbury Printing Company Ltd, Salisbury

Frontispiece illustration: Blacksmith at work outside Dewey's Forge, Donhead St Andrew, 1940s (detail from photograph reproduced on page 105).

Contents

NOTE: *The colour pages (between 64 and 65) have been included to show recent images of village buildings. In the main text many images are from old photographs which do not therefore show houses in their present state of repair.*

Foreword

FROM AN EARLY AGE I was interested in history and the world about me. In the late 1980s I started research into this beautiful place where we live – the Donheads. My request for the loan of old photographs to copy received an excellent response and I soon amassed a large archive of material. I put this to use by taking modern pictures to go with the old and produced a slide show with two projectors, *Donhead Then and Now*. Assisted by Diana Goetz, who reads passages for me during the show, we have given three performances at Donhead St Mary Village Hall and to several groups locally. I also produced a second show, *Ludwell Then and Now*, for the children at Ludwell School, and I have been very encouraged and surprised at the interest taken by the pupils.

A number of times I have been asked: 'Are you going to put it in a book?' But although I would have liked to do so I didn't know how to start – and anyway, as I told those who asked, I am an outdoor person, not a writer. One of these people was Anna McDowell, who said that she would be willing to scan all my slides and put them on to discs. I went up to her cottage almost every Friday morning from January to September (2005) doing a fixed number each week, and by the time I returned the following week she had typed up all the captions. Without her this would never have got off the ground, and I am eternally grateful to her.

So what next? I drifted on for a while and then Michael Coward approached me and said he would be willing to write an introduction and various headings, such as 'Schools', etc. Michael, assisted by Christine Speak, spent many hours into his part of the project. Anna had suggested that we should talk to John Chandler and we had a meeting to discuss the project. He told us that we needed someone with writing experience to help us and suggested Rex Sawyer. I have been friendly with Rex for a long time, so was pleased with this arrangement. We gave him a list of Donhead people to interview, which he did with great efficiency, and lent us his advice and expertise.

Here then is the result: *Donhead Past and Present*. Many thanks to all local people who have lent photographs and anecdotes, and have welcomed me into their homes and gardens.

Davⅰd McLean
June 2007

Introduction

DONHEAD lies in the extreme south-west corner of Wiltshire, on the edge of Salisbury Plain and Cranborne Chase. The parishes of Donhead St Andrew and Donhead St Mary are together known simply as 'The Donheads' or 'Donhead' and are here thought of as one unit. Donhead means 'head of the downs' – the chalk downs – which run westward from Salisbury Plain before the land dips steeply down into the Blackmore Vale beyond Shaftesbury.

Seen from Win Green (the highest point of the area at 277 metres) Donhead almost resembles a large, open saucer, with chalk in the south and east, and greensand in the west and north. Standing on Win Green, a magnificent view over the parishes of Donhead St Andrew and Donhead St Mary stretches in front – Donhead in all its glory. Large arable fields sweep smoothly from the chalk scarp but in the distance they give way to pasture and woodland and little hidden valleys cut by six of the tributaries of the River Nadder. It must be one of the most beautiful views in the south of England.

At the time when forest and woodland covered most of the lowland in Britain, early hunter gatherers would have used the drier chalk and greensand hills as route ways and later herdsmen would have settled on the slopes of these hills. There is evidence of Neolithic and Bronze Age occupation in Donhead. In the vicinity of the Ox Drove, Win Green and Charlton there are several barrows and Neolithic flint scrapers and flakes have been found near the springs of the Nadder, suggesting Neolithic people had settled there. Bronze Age tools also have been found near Castle Rings which is probably the site of a fortified Bronze Age camp.

Win Green with bonfire for King George V's silver jubilee celebrations.

One Roman road crosses the area from the south coast travelling towards Bath and it is possible that the commanding site of the present St Mary's Church was a meeting place from earliest times. Roman pottery of the second century AD was found on the site and there is a probable Roman well in a nearby garden.

After King Alfred founded a nunnery in Shaftesbury in 888 the Abbey soon acquired lands in Donhead and beyond. An area of land called 'the Donheads' in Shaftesbury Abbey's estate was the second most highly taxed in the Dunworth Hundred in 1334 and the sixth most highly rated in Wiltshire. In the same area in 1377 there were 359 poll tax payers, a number second only to Tisbury, so Donhead seems to have been fairly prosperous. Indeed, Donhead has always been a pleasant place to live and seems, particularly in the eighteenth and nineteenth centuries, to have encouraged many of the rich and famous to come and live here and to beautify the landscape by planting well designed parks and woodland to surround their large houses.

Beating the Bounds

A S THE ENGLISH parish boundaries evolved – and for the most part they had probably assumed a pattern fairly familiar to us today by about the tenth century – each parish tried as far as possible to include different types of land. Ideally, each needed some water meadows for early spring grass, some drier ground for cereals and roots, with hill grazing for the sheep and cattle in late summer. For example, Whitesheet Hill, in the south-east of the parish, provided hill grazing for Ansty, Donhead and Berwick St John.

Donhead St Mary claims to be the third largest parish in Wiltshire and encompasses some 2,115 hectares. St Andrew is smaller – 1,153 hectares. They adjoin a total of 11 other parishes. There is no real centre to Donhead for it is two very spread out parishes and the lack of a focal point has always been a problem. So we will start on the outside, at a place where we can see the whole of Donhead and where looking north, except in the far distance, almost everything we can see is Donhead. This spot is, of course, where the Roman road from Badbury Rings comes over the top of Win Green. Imagine a column of Roman soldiers marching over the crest! Coming over the crown of the hill and facing north gives a breath-taking view.

On the southern slopes of Win Green the boundary of Donhead meets Ashmore (the highest village in Dorset with a famous pond in the middle of its postcard setting). This is also the county boundary which runs along the road to Zig Zag Hill, dropping down into Melbury Abbas and Cann Common and then northwards, leaving Shaftesbury to the west. This famous Saxon hill-top town was the place where King Alfred founded his abbey. For nearly six centuries the abbey exerted a great influence over Donhead as it held land there, extending north-eastward to beyond Tisbury, where the Tithe Barn still stands. Shaftesbury is still the nearest shopping and service centre for most of the area.

At Littledown the parish boundary leaves the county boundary where it borders Motcombe, turns east and joins with Semley parish boundary along the top of the hill. The boundary with Semley encloses the ancient hill fort of Castle Rings in Donhead, which was probably a Bronze Age camp since tools of that time were found nearby. Here a circular field enclosure is surrounded by double banks which presumably had paling stakes at the top with a lower ditch on the outside. They are now covered with vegetation and most signs of occupation have been erased by farming. It was well protected from the weather and invaders. There are four entrances – now merely gaps in the earthworks – north. south, east and west which may or may not be original. There are also some signs of an outlying bank and ditch defence with the ditch facing west, suggesting that attack may have come from the west along the greensand ridge, perhaps from the direction of Shaftesbury and Win Green.

Castle Rings, 4.5 hectares surrounded by a deep ditch and a circle of trees.

Eastwards the boundary follows the delightfully named footpath called Tittle Path, marked on the old maps as Tickle Path, ending in Donhead Clift and continues on to Gutch Common. From Gutch Common ancient and recent common land stretches up to Barkers Hill. (This is probably a corruption of Bartholomew's Hill) This area of Donhead may well have remained as common grazing long after most of the land was enclosed with large fields and hedges around 1800. From Barker's Hill, which had a late nineteenth century Roman Catholic Chapel until a few years ago, the land falls to the Vale of

Wardour. This has been the home and family seat of the Arundell family since about 1500. At the time of the dissolution of the Abbey they were given extensive tracts of land in Donhead, much of which they retained until the middle of the twentieth century.

Wardour lies in the parish of Tisbury so Donhead St Andrew touches Tisbury. The parish boundary runs right through the middle of Old Wardour Castle to fields beyond, where it joins with Ansty – the village with its maypole still intact and the home of St John's Hospitallers, started in the thirteenth century. From Ansty the boundary crosses Whitesheet Hill to run with the parish of Berwick St John, at the head of the Chalke Valley. In the past a small area of Berwick St John was part of Donhead and known as Easton Bassett or Easton Basin. The boundary continues through the middle of Ferne Park and House up over the downs back to Win Green, to give Donhead St Andrew some more hill grazing, before it drops down into Ashgrove Bottom. Here it joins up with Tollard Royal (with its royal hunting lodge of Cranborne Chase) and then meets the Dorset border and Ashmore again.

Looking at the parish boundary, it seems strange that Ashgrove is in the parish of Donhead. One might think that the boundary would run along the Ox Drove, on the top of the hill, to the county boundary. There seems, however, to have been some confusion as early as 1122, in Henry I's reign, but by the dissolution of the monasteries it was judged to be in the manor of Donhead and so it passed to Sir Thomas Arundell, in 1574. Three other small detours in the parish boundaries are very interesting. It seems that the parish boundary between Donhead St Andrew and Donhead St Mary had been drawn up by the late eleventh century to make a detour through the middle of the demesne farmhouse, Lower Berrycourt. Legal cases pertaining to both parishes could be tried in one place. Payment of tithes might have been important here and also at Old Wardour Castle where the boundary runs through the middle of the castle. Another detour in the parish boundaries is where it goes right out of its way to include the spring at Rowberry – Donhead St Andrew really needed that water! The availability of water for domestic use and for watering cattle and sheep has always been of great importance in daily living. The flow of water could also be harnessed for power.

Village and Hamlet

THE POPULATION of Donhead (about 2,000) is scattered over the two parishes. Except for Charlton, there is no large nucleated village and settlement tends to be very dispersed, with many hamlets and much linear settlement. Farms mostly grew up along the roads with their fields stretching out around or behind them. Their workers' cottages were also built along the roads and one hamlet merges into another, with concentrations of settlement around the churches and at crossroads. This scattering of people has meant that in many ways it is difficult to foster a sense of social cohesion as there is no focal point. There is, nevertheless, a very strong sense of identity and pride in belonging to Donhead!

The only example of a nucleated village, **Charlton**, lies in a shallow basin of its own with most of the houses close together along the single village street. Charlton is a very good example of an old medieval village, with Home Farm being at the centre with its open stock yard, a fourteenth century church, with a village pond just across the road and water meadows below. If the road is traced round from Middle Farm up to Manor Farm, then around the Charlton Lanes to what was Spring Farm and on to what is now the Remembrance Field and Charlton House, all the Home Farm fields can

Manor House, now Charlton House, 1920s

be seen spreading out from the central farm house. It formed a tight village community from about the tenth to the eighteenth centuries.

Home Farm, 1912

At night the sheep were shut up in portable hurdle pens on the cereal fields partly for safety reasons but mainly to fertilize the ground. By day they were allowed up on to the common grazing fields and hills to feed, while their night pen was moved.

It was not until about 1750 that the open common grazing fields were enclosed and agriculture became more intensive. This was partly brought about by an increase in urban population which needed food. Many new ideas then came into farming with new breeds of livestock, new fodder crops and new machinery. It was Mr Robert Graves, from London, who bought most of the land at Charlton from 1823, built Charlton House in 1850 and built Manor Farm, Charlton as a 'model farm' to try out all the new ideas in farming. This pattern was repeated on other estates up and down the country at this time. Charlton church was pulled down in 1839 as it was not large enough for the congregation. A new church was built up by the main road to which Mr Graves contributed generously.

Across the meadows from Charlton a delightful spring emerges from under a large rock near the village of **Ludwell**. This is one source of the Nadder. This warm, clear water is almost immediately used to grow watercress. Mr R. W. Williamson started growing watercress in 1893 on the site of 'Charlton Mill'. It found a ready market in London when the

Charlton Church, demolished 1839

railway came through to Semley station, after 1859. Today it has been greatly reduced but some is still grown. Another use for this water was to work the hydraulic ram near the spring which pumped water to all the Charlton estate farms in the neighbourhood. In the early part of the twentieth century there were several of these rams in Donhead. The withy beds which formerly provided the material for basket making can still be seen.

Rossiters butchers shop, 1920s.

The stream then runs under the A30. Where the water crosses under the road horses and carts used to come in dry summers, to haul water around Donhead and even back up over Win Green to Ashmore to water the sheep when the village pond went dry. In dry weather the wooden wagon wheels dried out in the metal bond and had to be soaked in the river to 'plimm' them up.

Within living memory a wagon works existed at Birdbush and there were also two chapels and a pub, the Lamb, but these are all now closed. Mr Rossiter used to have a butcher's shop and also a dairy farm. He would deliver milk all round the village using a pony and trap with a seventeen gallon churn on it. He would ladle the milk into customers' own jugs. There was a tailor's shop (owned by Mr Gatehouse) and the workmen could be seen sitting cross-legged on their tables doing the sewing. Below the current Post Office was a bakery providing daily bread. Behind the shop the barber would come some evenings a week to give hair-cuts. Just before the river Mr Jack Sansom had his garage for cars and general repairs. The workhouse, a three-storey building, was opposite the Grove Arms but closed when Tisbury Union took over in 1868 from the local poor house and moved the inmates to Tisbury. Graves can be found in St Mary's churchyard with the words 'Inmate of Tisbury Union' on them. Grove House Hotel (now a private house) was a nursing home.

Ludwell Hollow, early 1900s.

Ludwell is a street village with buildings lining the main road and is now joined with the hamlet of Birdbush. Only three buildings are now shops: there is an excellent Post Office and General Stores, a dressmaker's shop and also a first class butcher's shop. Ludwell can almost be thought of as Donhead's industrial focus, not only now but over many centuries. Two farms now

Young Tom Rossiter in the 1960s. He still farms at Birdbush.

remain, one at Peckons Hill and another at Birdbush. Only one pub remains – the Grove Arms in Ludwell Bottom.

Ludwell Hollow must be able to tell many a story with the Grove Arms at the bottom and the Rising Sun at the top! There is an account of how on one occasion when Lady Grosvenor was travelling from Motcombe House, the shaft on her coach broke on the hill and she had to wait for a replacement to be brought from Motcombe before she could continue her journey. The gradient of the hill was eased in the 1960s, making it more friendly.

At the top of the hill the church of St John's dominates the skyline with its twin towers. The Old Remembrance Hall was built before 1840 and Ludwell School in 1875. Nearby, the Coronation Drive estate was built after the war in the 1950s and St John's Close was later tucked in behind the church and the Old Remembrance Hall. Within this area

The old Remembrance Hall, 1970s.

of about 6 hectares is found a quarter of the parish's population. The New Remembrance Hall was opened in 1990 and the Old Remembrance Hall was sold. The new hall is across the A30, next to the Sports Centre and playing fields. Dewey Close has recently been built and Smithy House now marks the site of an old thatched cottage where the village blacksmith, Jimmy Randall, used to live. His blacksmith's shop was down in Charlton Village.

Travelling from St John's along the A30, here called Salisbury Road,

Jimmy Randall working during the 1950s outside his thatched cottage where Deweys Close is now.

Coombe House.

there are scattered houses along the side. But north of the road is a part of Donhead like no other – the **Coombes**. This is a lovely, quiet, narrow valley cut into by another of the headwaters of the Nadder, its slopes covered with trees. The stream has been dammed in several places to form lakes of varying sizes, which add to the peace and beauty of the valley and also aid wild life. There are three little hamlets, Upper, Middle and Lower Coombe, with small clusters of houses along the very narrow lanes. The valley starts at Coombe House, built in 1886, by Mark Beaufoy MP, a vinegar manufacturer from Barnsley, who owned 251 hectares when he died in 1922. A little further down the valley stands Coombe Priory, an old seventeenth century farmhouse, much enlarged in the twentieth century. It belonged to the Roman Catholic Arundell family and gets its name from when Lord Arundell sheltered five Carthusian monks from the French Revolution. In Donhead St

Coombe Priory, 1930s.

Lower Coombe Farm in 1926.

Mary Church there is a wall tablet at the base of the tower (on the south side) dedicated to Dom Anthelm Guillaume of Bourdon, Normandy, who died at Coombe Priory in 1798, aged 88. They sought refuge in what was then a very remote area. At Lower Coombe Farm at the end of the valley there are three stones to mark members of the Pond family who died of the plague in 1665. A word of warning, do not venture down these lanes in a large car!.

Graves of the Pond family dated 1665.

It is interesting to note that during much of the nineteenth century most of the land in the southern part of Donhead St Mary was owned by just three families: the Beaufoys, who also owned most of the Coombes, the Graves who owned most of Charlton and the Groves who owned Ferne, Higher Berrycourt and all the land down to Ludwell.

A wonderful view greets the walker climbing out of the Coombes where there is a house named Windwhistle – very aptly named when the north-east wind blows. From there the land drops steeply to the **Wincombe** valley. Here is

Donhead St Mary church showing Mr Samson and the bellringers.

said to be the real source of the Nadder, but it is only a collection of very small springs which flow into a man-made lake. Wincombe House was built about 1820, at the same time as Charlton House, which it resembles. The house and park stand at the head of the valley with a view that goes right down through Donhead.

The old village of **Donhead St Mary** is sited on a spur of greensand. It is different from Charlton both in its site and position and also because, from very early times, the whole spur was owned by and run for the Church. The fields on either side of the road were glebe fields belonging to the church for the use of the rector, or providing rent to the church. There were also glebe fields along Britmore Lane. There was no suitably dry land for cereal growing or grazing large numbers of sheep, but there was probably open common land beyond, as far as Gutch Common where there is a small hamlet.

Many of the original houses depended on the church and the services it offered to travellers. It would appear to have been a centre of importance for quite a large area. Pilgrim's Cottage offered shelter to travellers and Shute House was originally a resting place for sick travellers, although later it became the Rectory. Everyone in the area round the church was concerned with the life of the church – it was a sort of close. All around are small cottages where employees of the church lived e.g. vergers, sacristans, housekeepers in the Rectory and stable hands. There was a village shop

Dunworth House, 1950s.

Mr Samson at the rear of Dunworth House, where he had his workshop and petrol pumps.

in 'The Old Stores' until the 1980s, a library in what was an old school and the village school was in what is now the Village Hall. At Dunworth House there were petrol pumps.

The pattern of fields centring on Church Hill Farm opposite the church does show some similarity with Charlton, with a 'ring road' down Church Hill, along Watery Lane up to Jenkins Corner. It is not certain whether it all belonged to the church but until the 1970s all the agricultural land around, extending to half way along Britmore Lane, was glebe land. From the top of the church tower looking southwards down the hill, or when looking at a map, a different pattern from Charlton is seen: all the houses down both sides of Church Hill have long narrow strips of land sloping away from the houses. These strips of land were a householder's independence where he was able to grow his own food, graze his horse for his own cart or trap, and keep a pig and a few sheep for his family. Without this little strip of land or allotment all those householders would have been much poorer and less fulfilled. This way of life continued until the 1950s.

Burltons in the 1970s.

Glyn Farm, farmed
for many years by the
Burton family. It is
seen here in the 1950s.

(below) Burton
family off for a day's
shooting. late 1970s.

(left) The Malthouse, early 1900s.

The brewery behind Sunnybank (now Tulip Tree) in the mid- to late-1920s. When this was
demolished the stone was used to build a house down the road called 'Bruins' (brewery ruins).

Home Close.

Home Cottage, looking towards theMalthouse, 1950s.

Travelling down the hill one encounters houses of varying ages, the largest of which is Burltons, opposite Fair View Farm. Where the road meets the lane from Donhead St Andrew is a little hamlet with Glyn Farm, Home Close, Home Cottage and some newer houses. Where the road bends round, the imposing frontage of the Malthouse which once belonged to the brewery is seen and on the other side are Sunnybank Cottages, formerly Brewery Cottages. Below the Malthouse is the Methodist Chapel and opposite that the more modern house now called Bruins House but reputedly named 'Bruins' to mark the brewery ruins. Continuing down the hill is another hamlet, Lillies Green, of about seven old houses and some newer additions. At one time here was a blacksmith and a fish and chip shop at the fork in the road.

Members of the Jeffery family outside the Malthouse in the 1920s.

With all its valuable water Donhead had eight mills in 1086, the time of the Domesday Book, of which five were in St Mary. It is remarkable to think of all the work involved in channelling the water and constructing the dams and buildings strong enough to stand all the workings of mill machinery. Except for Mullins Mill, which was a fulling mill, they were probably all used for grinding wheat for bread-making for human consumption or other grains for animal feed. Horses needed oats and pigs needed barley. Possibly Shaftesbury Abbey used the Donhead mills as being the nearest and most easily reached. Ashmore and Berwick St John

Mullins Mill (once a fulling mill), seen here in 2000.

undoubtedly brought grain to Donhead for milling. The mills were Charlton Mill (probably by the A 30), Ludwell Mill (by the old Williamson's watercress beds), Mullins Mill and Donhead Hall Mill (at the bottom of Horsehills). There is now no sign of the fifth mill which was below Rose Cottage (Watery Lane).

Donhead Hall Mill in 2000.

In **Donhead St Andrew** there were three mills along the river. West End Mill, which lies along the border with Donhead St Mary, and Ricketts Mill still retain their mill features. Kelloways Mill was also one of the eight Domesday mills and both it and Ricketts Mill were still working in the early twentieth century.

Rose Cottage, Watery Lane, in the 1970s.

Settlement in Donhead St Andrew is more dispersed than in St Mary. There was no obvious old centre of settlement around the church. Houses are found at intervals up Bartholomew Street from the church, and similarly, to the south-

West End Mill in 2000.

east, beyond the cemetery, houses of mixed ages line the roads. The pub, the Forester, is found here. It was not until the second half of the twentieth century that Donhead St Andrew really had a centre. Behind the church, on what was Donhead House Farm several new houses were built in the 1990s. The area opposite the Forester was built up and just over Cross Bridges a new group of houses has been developed. This has greatly

West End Mill, still retaining the cogs and gear wheels – the teeth are made of applewood.

assisted in building a stronger sense of community in what was a very scattered settlement. These developments have quite definitely altered the shape and structure of the village. There is a large estate at each end of the parish, Wardour at the north end and Ferne to the south.

Nearby was Mansfield Farm, an example of twentieth century change. The farm was about 20 hectares, over the bridge towards Beauchamp House and Pigtrough Lane. Mansfield farmhouse was just at the side of the old crooked bridge. It stood where there is now a swimming pool. During the war the Arundell family let it to the Red Cross as a house for convalescent soldiers, but after the war it was considered to be in too rough a condition and it was pulled down.

Most of the farmyard was taken over by Dewey's Transport which started by hauling coal and other goods from Tisbury Station, but soon expanded to 20 or 30 lorries hauling goods all over the country. The lorries were considered too large for the Donhead Lanes so the fleet of lorries was moved down to the old airfield at Henstridge and the old garage site was made available for building – peace has been restored to a quiet cul-de-sac.

Kelloways Mill in 2000.

Ricketts Mill in 2000.

Pigtrough Lane is delightfully named and marks the end of the village to the east although there is another hamlet along Sands Lane. At Sands Farm there were 120 acres of glebe land. Sheep were the main product of farming from the fifteenth to the eighteenth centuries and at one time there were 2000 sheep in the parish. The barn just off Sands Lane is called the Drove Barn, a reflection of the use to which it was put. Over the other side of the Dengrove valley, towards the top of Gould's Farm is the cottage called Little Shepherd's Shelter, where a shepherd could have spent a warm, dry night close to his sheep. The Dengrove valley itself has recently been the site of a trout farm, using the clear, warm water of the spring there.

West End, with several new houses, links the main part of the village to Overway and Milkwell with a hamlet of several old houses at the junction of the road to St Mary. In Milkwell there are several older houses but the south end of Overway is mostly post-war.

Roads and tracks

EVER SINCE HUMANS have been in this area – some five or six thousand years – they have travelled around seeking food, water and shelter. They travelled first on foot, then on horse or donkey and then by cart or carriage. Small settlements grew up. Paths and tracks evolved to link these hamlets and would join up at centres of commerce, defence and worship. Only during the last 80 years has the motor car been available to almost everyone, completely changing our pattern of life. But the motor car and its need for wide roads has not yet had too much effect on Donhead's road pattern. The roads are basically still the same as the cart tracks that made them, the famous Donhead Lanes, well known for mystifying travellers! (As a youngster the author was lucky enough to have driven a horse and cart along these lanes – although he did not think so at the time!) Horses do not like walking in a straight line but prefer the expectation of something around the next corner. So we have the intriguing network of lanes that join up all our hamlets, coming together to cross the six streams which together make up the Nadder, and following wherever possible the contours of the hills. It is remarkable how mercifully little influence the motor car has had on the main pattern of lanes in Donhead. More roads have, in fact, been closed than opened up.

Three ancient tracks run through the Donheads. The Roman Road from Badbury Rings to Bath comes into the parish of St Mary just west of Win Green (where it can be traced to the west of the present road). There is actually no other place on the downs where this crossroads could be, as there are two steep valleys to the south and east which prohibited any roadway; on the north facing

(left) The Roman road crosses the A30 next to the house that was the Lamb Inn, where this milestone stands. (above) Roman well in the garden of a house below Donhead St Mary church near the course of the Roman road.

slope the road follows a spur, the only place where the gradient is more gentle. It passes down through Dennis Lane in Birdbush and can then be seen just above Lower Berrycourt Farm. It crosses the stream, passing to the west of the Methodist Chapel, then up to and east of St Mary's Church. From there it follows the line of Berrywood Lane, through the gap to Gutch Common and on into Semley, eventually passing through East Knoyle and Longleat to Bath.

A second ancient track is the Ox Drove which runs along the top of the chalk hills to Win Green, and was probably used by the earliest travellers to avoid the forested lowlands. It is a track with wide verges either side to take a large number of sheep. In medieval times it was mainly used for driving large flocks of sheep and cattle from the Blackmore Vale to Fairs at Wilton, Britford, Cold Berwick Hill (Hindon), Chilmark and possibly beyond. Drovers were a special breed and knew the routes and where food, water and night pens could be found.

The third track is the coach road from Salisbury via the Race Course and along another range of hills for about 25 kilometres to Whitesheet Hill. This was an ideal route for centuries along a hard, dry, reasonably level, surface. It avoided the rivers and marshy land and was used by stage and mail coaches as well as all commercial and private travel. As the value of the mail and private travel became greater so the highwaymen could very easily take their pickings on the isolated hillside and it became necessary, therefore, to build a bridge across the Nadder at Barford St Martin (where there was undoubtedly already a locally used ford) and continue the road along the line of the present A30.

Milestone on a track above Whitesheet.

Thereafter it bypasses all the villages keeping close to the downs. The top road ceased to be a turnpike in 1864.

At the top of the hill with its wonderful views is an ancient milestone that reads:

SALISBURY XIV MILES: HYDE PARK CORNER
XCVII MILES
1736

Here the old coach road descends into Donhead. On the hill is a old lime works (disused from 1946) and below is Arundell Farm. This used to be called The Glove Inn and was where they changed the horses before or after the steep slope of Whitesheet Hill. (It must have been quite a business wondering what sort of horse you would get next!) Russian Comfrey is often found at the bottom of these hills to give the horses extra high protein and energy for the climb.

About 100 metres west of the Glove Inn was an important cross roads where the route from Salisbury to Shaftesbury crossed the road from Donhead St Andrew to Berwick St John. It was mentioned in 1608. This is called Whitesands Cross (locally pronounced Whitsuns). If a traveller had made his way right through the Blackmore Vale in the wet winter months, over the Blackmore Vale Clay to Shaftesbury and along the road to Ludwell and Brookwater he would be cheered to arrive at the top of Brook Hill, with the view of White Sheet Hill, known as the White Sands, knowing there would then be 15 miles of flat, dry land all the way to Salisbury. (The names Whitesands Cross and Sands Lane all refer to the white chalk hills).

Road descending from Whitesheet.

From Whitesands Cross the coach road (now the A30) moves into Brookwater down a steep incline over the bridge into Donhead St Mary and up the other side to Birdbush, Ludwell and Shaftesbury. Heavily laden wagons would probably have gone round by Rowberry, Ferne Wall and Charlton to avoid the three steep hills.

After the bottom of White Sheet Hill is reached many smaller roads, such as Sands Lane, lead off from the old coach road which was the centre of travel for so many centuries and, therefore formed the backbone of our villages' road pattern. Near the *Glove Inn* Sands Lane takes a direct straight line, avoiding flooding, to Donhead Mill for milling the grain for bread making and animal feed. It all had to be hauled from the farms by horse there and back. The line of Sands Lane continues through to Hatch and Pythouse the home of the Benett family who held great influence over that area. The Arundells of Wardour would

John and Gordon Popham farmed at Castle Farm, Lower Wincombe Lane from the 1940s and were a backbone of village life. They are seen here together in the 1960s (left); Gordon is driving a tractor in the 1940s (right). They both died in June 2007 and at their memorial service the following tribute by Maureen Bone was read to the mourners.

'As long as I can remember there have always been the "Pops" at Castle Farm. Whenever you called, the welcome was warm. The table in the farmhouse was spread with goodies and the teapot was ready for action! The family had such infectious good humour – nothing daunted their spirits. They worked hard to produce good land and stock of the highest quality. In Donhead and surrounding areas Gordon and John commanded huge respect. Wherever there was a farming event or agricultural sales and shows, you could be sure to meet the Popham Brothers, sparkling with congenial remarks and timely advice if required. "The Boys" could relate to both young and old – there was always time for a chat and a chuckle, So many people benefited from their generosity and love. Nothing was too much trouble. They had time to listen; the day seemed to go so much better after a meeting with them. It was their zest and joy of living which inspired us all, truly remarkable brothers! Soul mates in life and death. It was a privilege to have known them both. Lower Wincombe Lane will be the poorer without Gordon and John; this is the end of ane era.'

Silage-making using the Dorset Wedge system at Castle Farm, Lower Wincombe, 1940s.

have left the coach road earlier, at Ansty, and gone directly over the down to what is now the Polo Field and then through Horwood Park to Wardour Castle.

Three other old tracks deserve a mention. From Cross Bridges, heading eastwards out of Donhead St Andrew, Wardour Lane crossed straight over Sands Lane to Pile Oak Cottage and went down through Wardour Park, between two of the lakes. This was probably a very busy road at one time, taking horse-drawn traffic from Shaftesbury to Wardour. When Wardour Park was created in the eighteenth century New Road was cut through to form a new main road skirting the park, and the old track went out of use. Similarly, another track, no longer used, went from Middle Coombe up over to Windwhistle. From there it dropped down into Wincombe valley and up to Castle Rings. This track was taken out of use when Wincombe House was built, the lake constructed and the area turned into parkland. Perhaps the Lower Wincombe Road, which comes to an abrupt end at Lower Wincombe, joined this road. A third track runs across Charlton Fields. Starting by the Remembrance Field and going due south, a track leads to Cann Common and Melbury Abbas. This track was used as a bridleway until fairly recently to join Donhead with Melbury and Cann.

Churches and Places of Worship

PARTS OF **St Andrew's Church** date back to the ninth and tenth centuries. The church is very low lying and the river is very close. It is interesting to surmise what the surroundings looked like when it was first built. When Kelloways Mill (below the church) was working the water would have been held up to get the level of water to drive the water wheel. Before Donhead House was built, or indeed the wall around the house was put up, the view across the fields to the south-west must have been magnificent. (It was probably Horace Chapman who put up the wall when he bought the rectory in 1895.) Today St Andrew's church is almost overshadowed by the new houses nearby.

From the ninth century St Andrew's Church was under the patronage of Shaftesbury Abbey. One small piece of medieval glass survives (now embedded in the top of the east window) depicting the arms of the Abbey. After the dissolution of the monasteries the patronage passed to Sir Thomas Arundell of Wardour Castle. There has always been a high proportion of Roman Catholics in the parish, probably due to its close connections with, and proximity to, Wardour.

Like most village churches, St Andrew's has been enlarged over the centuries, the side aisles being added in the fourteenth and fifteenth centuries. The chancel was taken down and rebuilt in 1833 and the present tower was built out of old materials towards the end of the nineteenth century.

A moving feature of the church, thought to be unique in England, is the face of Christ supporting the springing of the arch at the west end. His brow is

Donhead St Andrew church in the 1960s.

lined with sorrow and the eyes are gazing wistfully towards the altar. A very attractive feature of the church is a series of medieval carved angels high up on either side of the nave. Some have musical instruments such as lutes. At the restoration of the tower some fragments, perhaps of Viking origin, were built into the inside wall. There are four bells in the tower, one dating from the fifteenth century, and the wooden beams that hold the bells are very old.

The windows were put into the chancel when it was refurbished in 1833 by the Revd. William Dansey and his family. He was rector from 1820 to 1856 and it was he who was responsible for starting the village school.

At the west end of the church is a very fine stained glass window created by Henry Haig, depicting the baptism of fire and the Holy Spirit. This was installed by the Friends of St Andrew's to mark the Millennium. There is a very fine prayer book holder and money box in memory of the Revd. John Godfrey (1954-1976) who died in 1980. Two priests' chairs were also made by Phil Thorp a local craftsman.

There is a very interesting wall tablet to Captain John Cooke who lived at Donhead Lodge, just across the river, and who was killed at the battle of Trafalgar. His ship, the Bellerophon, later took Buonaparte to his final captivity in St Helena.

The list of Rectors in the parish (to be seen in the church) is interesting: there were 12 in the fourteenth century (with three in 1302), eleven in the fifteenth century, five in the sixteenth, and three in the seventeenth century, excluding J. Legg, a 'Commonwealth intruder'. In the eighteenth century there were only two. but there were six in the nineteenth and five in the twentieth.

St Mary's Church occupies a commanding position at the end of a greensand bluff. Wherever one is in the Donheads, St Mary's Church stands out right in the centre of things like a candle in the middle of our Donhead saucer! Almost certainly it has been a place of worship, and perhaps a site for sacrificial rites, dating back to earliest times. With its wide ranging views across to Win Green and over the valley of the Nadder it may also have been a defended site. Coincidentally (or is it coincidence?) three almost straight lines joining places of historical and natural interest appear to converge on the triangle immediately below St Mary's Church. The first, maybe originating only as a footpath or bridleway, runs straight from Shaftesbury Abbey to Donhead St Mary Church. It continues straight down to St Andrew's Church, through to Old Wardour Castle and Castle Ditches at Tisbury. North-eastwards, the line goes through the churchyard at Stapleford and straight on to

Donhead St Mary church in the 1970s.

Stonehenge. From Shaftesbury Abbey it runs south-west to Cerne Abbas and Punchknowle Beacon (a hill on the south coast).

Another probable track way, originating at Glastonbury passes through Castle Rings, continues past St Mary's and via Whitesands Cross goes to Winklebury Hill Fort and on through Martin Down, Bokerly Ditch and great Roman encampments, perhaps on to Southampton. The third line is the Roman Road from Badbury Rings to Bath, which passes up the eastern side of the church, by High Bank, meeting the road which comes from Castle Rings. These three roads or tracks all cross over at the triangle immediately below St Mary's Church.

This area, not far from the Shute spring with its clear water for cleansing and refreshment, undoubtedly formed a meeting point for prayer and worship over many centuries. There may well have been a prayer cross on the triangle below the church in medieval times where weary travellers could put down their bundles and sit to gossip! There was almost certainly a wooden frame church built on the spot in Saxon times, but the first building of which there is any evidence was probably a stone built single nave church in Norman times in the eleventh century. As in many churches around the country it gradually expanded, adding aisles and a chancel in succeeding centuries.

When King Alfred built his abbey in Shaftesbury he installed his thirteen-year old daughter as the first Abbess and dedicated his abbey to the Virgin Mary. It is not surprising, therefore, that so many of the sister churches to the abbey were dedicated to St Mary.

Climbing up the hill through the fields to the east of the church the scene is dominated by the chancel, nave and tower: its churchyard has several old yew trees and graves commemorating former residents. There are several small old, thatched cottages tucked into the slope at the bottom and to the west of the church, the houses of former church servants. The whole church is built of local greensand (although when some cornerstones had to be repaired in the late 1980s the nearest match came from Alsace). At the west end of the church is a tower which has clearly been added to at different times. The blocked window in the tower wall suggests that the tower was built before the nave was raised. The bottom part is probably fourteenth century. The top is decorated with four corner pinnacles and four in the intervening spaces.

On the outside of the tower on the south side can be seen the marks of the pointed roof line of a priest's house which was attached to the church before the reformation. This was entered through a door (now blocked) at the west end of the south aisle and was probably removed in the sixteenth century, perhaps during the Reformation. The priest would have been on hand for his daily offices, morning noon and evening

On either side of the porch are two boot scrapers – as there are outside many old buildings. They are reminiscent of a different kind of congregation from that of today. One hundred and fifty years ago most people walked across the fields and footpaths to get to church and it would be unthinkable to carry the mud into church. Probably the yew tree branches were laid on the floor to take up much of the mud. The attractive, vaulted fourteenth century porch itself is now the home of twenty-first century bats!

The Norman font.

Stepping down into the church through the old oak door, the visitor is struck by the light airy interior. The nave was heightened and given clerestory windows in the thirteenth century and the choir stalls, vestry and organ were moved in the 1950s thus enhancing the feeling of space and light, helped by the plain glass in the windows of the side aisles. The Norman font, with carving around the top and sides, which faces the visitor on entering the church, dates from the eleventh century. To quote from Skelton p 32: 'It has a wonderful aura with a strong physical sense of time passing'. On the south side of the north aisle there is a small piece of frieze which perhaps dates back to the twelfth century. The pulpit is restored Jacobean.

First the south and then the north aisles were added in the twelfth or thirteenth century to 'complete' the church. There are three bay arcades and the carving on the tops of the columns in the north and south aisles are interestingly different, the former being plain and the latter carved. The present, enlarged chancel probably dates from the fifteenth century. It is linked by open arches to the side chapels which are probably of fourteenth century origin, thus increasing the feeling of space. The whole church gives a feeling of many centuries of worship and loving care.

The glass is good, mostly of the nineteenth century. The east window dates from the 1880s and was dedicated to Richard Blackmore, a former rector. (In the church accounts of Donhead St Mary with Charlton there still exists an interesting entry referring to the Blackmore Charity Fund. In 1882 the Revd. R.W. Blackmore gave £500 the interest on which was to be given to the Coal Club to buy coal to be distributed to the poor of the parish to help with winter heating. In 1900-1901 £12 was used to buy 16 tons of coal which was distributed to 39 households all of whom made a small payment for each hundredweight received. This record is fascinating as it meant 16 tons of coal had to be brought from Tisbury Station. One good horse on its own could pull 5 or 6 hundredweight back to Donhead in one trip. Two loads a day could be taken if the driver got up early enough in the morning. That job is therefore a month's work for one man and his horse after harvest. Such stories illustrate a different life when the only form of transport was a horse. The fund still remains in the accounts for the interest to be paid to the Sunday School – if it existed.)

The windows in the north chapel were probably done by the well-known glass painter and designer, Charles Kempe, in the 1860s. Apparently Kempe wished to be ordained but as he stuttered he was refused ordination. He performed his ministry through his stained glass windows, employing 150 men nationally. The west window of the nave is dedicated to the Revd. Thomas Warburton Dunston. The window in the south chapel was designed and made by Henry Haig and is dedicated to Frederick Warburton Dunston, his wife and children. One of the family 'Miss Dunston', who lived at Burltons with her brother and niece, was an awe-inspiring lady, active in the village until the 1960s. (A head and shoulders drawing of her is in the Village Hall.) The window which combines skills of painting, staining, and etching of glass, was dedicated in 1984. Its use of blue is striking.

There are many memorial tablets to notable members of the village families including the Grove family, Boulay and Wyndham both of Donhead Hall, Maria Gordon of Wincombe Park, and W Purvis who died at Donhead Hall while visiting his friend Godfrey Kneller. The oldest tablet (recently restored) is to John Jeffries, born 1654, died 1713. The most unusual is a tablet in the current vestry at the west end of the church, which records the death of a priest from Normandy who had sought refuge with other monks in the Coombes.

> ### D. O. M.
> DOM. ANTHELM GUILLEMET.
>
> A CARTHUSIAN MONK.
>
> OF THE CONVENT OF BOURBON
>
> IN NORMANDY.
>
> BANISHED FROM HIS COUNTRY
>
> FOR RELIGION.
>
> HE DIED AT COOMB
>
> APRIL 27TH 1798
>
> IN THE 84TH YEAR OF HIS AGE
>
> AND 55TH YEAR OF HIS PROFESSION
>
> MAY HE REST IN PEACE
>
> AMEN
>
> HE DIED IN A GOOD AGE.
>
> FULL OF DAYS. GEN 25 8 V.

In the twenty-first century there is a very strong team of bell ringers ranging in age from eight to nearly eighty. The peal of six bells is considered to be of high quality and complimented by teams of visiting ringers who include them in their tour of church towers. Number four bell has an inscription

R WELLS OF ALDBOURNE FECIT MDCCLXXI

and the number six bell is inscribed

IN CHEERFUL NOTES WITH ONE ACCORD
WE SIX WILL IOIN TO PRAISE THE LORD

St John's Charlton is a comparatively modern church. The old fourteenth century Chapel of Ease at Charlton was pulled down in 1839 to be replaced by a bigger, modern, open plan church on the crossroads between Charlton and Donhead and the main A30 road. The old church was considered too small for the growing congregation and the site on the crossroads was chosen to make it more accessible to people from Ludwell and the Coombes.

It cost £1765, the money to build it being raised by public subscription although Mr Graves from Charlton House, probably made a considerable contribution and had quite a say in its building. The story goes that he had two wives and he built two towers in their memories. Hence it is known as the church with two towers. (Another story is that it is supposed to have been inspired by Notre Dame in Paris.) The sanctuary is the full width of the church. This allows the altar to have full width drapes with candlesticks to each side which sets off the most important place in the church to its best.

St John's church, Charlton in 2000.

Interior of St John's.

The east wall has a central window depicting some of the apostles while the windows to the left and right are of Mary and Martha. These were given by Mr Richard Hedges in memory of his first wife, Fiona. Mr Hedges also contributed generously to St John's Church when it was modernised in the 1960s. New under floor heating was installed and the organ was moved from the east end to the balcony. (The church is now heated by new gas heating.) The parish War Memorial is in St John's Churchyard along with many interesting grave stones. St John's is in the middle of the most densely populated part of Donhead with houses now surrounding it on all sides, and the New Remembrance Hall and Remembrance Field just across the A30.

The Roman Catholic Chapel The Arundells, who were prominent Roman Catholics, retained Jesuit priests at Wardour and there are a number of houses which have been used for their services. In the late eighteenth century

St John's choir in the 1950s.

there was considered to be 122 practising Roman Catholics in the parish. As the Arundells owned much of the land in Donhead for a long time many people have looked to Wardour as their spiritual centre over many centuries.

In 1891-2 the Revd. H. E. Chapman, then rector of St Andrew's, resigned his living, bought the rectory as his private house and became a Roman Catholic. It was on Chapman's initiative that a chapel dedicated to St Bartholomew was opened in 1887 on St Bartholomew's Hill. The chapel was served from Wardour and mass was said each Sunday from 1938-1960 when it closed.

Non-Conformist Chapels

There have been many licensed – and unlicensed! – meeting houses since 1650. Worship took place all over the village, even at the barn at Lower Berrycourt, and in the woods at Berrywood. Thomas Grove, at Ferne harboured many dissenters. Between 1750 and 1850 several chapels were built within the parish, Birdbush Congregational Church being the most important historically. The following extract, from *History of the Wilts and East Somerset Congregational Union* by Revd. S B Stribling, recounts its beginnings. (It is now closed and has been pulled down.)

> The Church at Birdbush, in the parish of Donhead St Mary, traces its origin to the labours of one of the ejected ministers of 1662, the Revd. Peter Ince, of Brasenose College, Oxford and who, previously to his being silenced, was Rector of Donhead St Mary. 'Not long after 1662 Mr. Grove, a gentleman of great opulence, whose seat (Ferne House, Donhead St Andrew), was near Birdbush, upon his wife's lying dangerously ill, sent to the parish minister to pray with her. When the message came, he was just going out with the hounds, and sent word he would come when the hunt was over. Mr. Grove expressing much resentment at this, one of the servants took the liberty of saying, 'Sir, our shepherd can pray very well, if you will send for him, for we have often heard him at prayer in the field'. Upon this he was immediately sent for, and Mr. Grove asking him whether he could pray, the shepherd replied, 'God forbid, sir,

that I should live one day without prayer.' Hereupon he was desired to pray with the sick lady, which he did so pertinently to her case, with such fluency and fervour of devotion, as greatly to astonish her husband and all the family who were present. When they arose from their knees, Mr. Grove said to him, 'Your language and manner discover you to be a different person than what your appearance indicates – tell me who and what you are, and what were your views and situation in life before you came into my service'. He then told him 'he was one of the clergy men lately ejected from the Church and having nothing of his own left he was content for a livelihood to submit to the honest and peaceful employment of tending sheep.' Upon hearing this, Mr. Grove said, 'Then you shall be my shepherd' and received him into his house. A congregation was then assembled in the house for worship (Mr Grove having from this become a Presbyterian), but on his death in 1691, they were obliged to obtain accommodation in the neighbouring parish of Donhead St Mary. After worshipping there for some years, and the danger of persecution having passed, a chapel was erected, in 1723 by the congregation, on ground presented by one of their number, on the spot where they then worshipped, and where the present chapel stands; and a Parsonage was afterwards added. But though the church at Birdbush traces its origins to the labours of Mr. Ince, the Revd. Edward Warren was the first accredited pastor of the congregation; and the original trust-deed of the Chapel declares that the meeting-house was erected 'for the use of a congregation of Protestant Dissenters called Presbyterians:' But the church afterwards became Independent, and exercised its own authority in the management of its affairs, Much might be added respecting Mr. Warren's high personal qualities and excellent ministry; and many other particulars might be given about the subsequent ministry of this Church, but space prevents. It is sufficient to say that the names of Groves and Ince are hallowed in this district, and but for the residence of Mr. Ince in this locality two centuries ago, the Church at Birdbush, humanly speaking, would not have had an existence.

Of the possible five non-conformist chapels that have existed, the **Wesleyan Methodist Chapel,** opened in 1837, on the lower part of Church Hill in Donhead St Mary, is the only one still open in the twenty-first century. When it was opened people came from far and wide to join

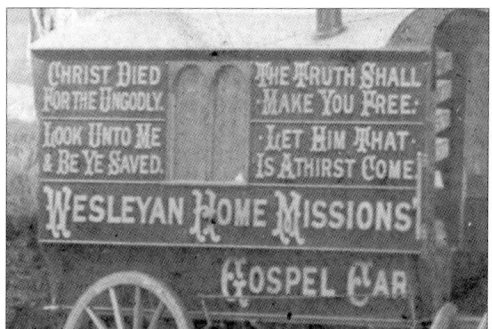

Early 1900s mobile wagon for imparting the gospel.

Donhead Methodist chapel, photographed in the 1890s or early 1900s.

in the festivities. The field around it was full with picnickers and ponies and traps. The head gardener at Donhead Hall was one of the prime movers in getting the chapel built and for many years afterwards the congregation of the chapel was allowed up to the gardens of Donhead Hall for a special treat each year. Like all places of worship it has been suffering from falling congregations in recent years but thanks to a few faithful worshippers it is still open in 2007. There were chapels at Barker's Hill, Ludwell and Charlton.

The Society of Friends ('the Quakers') do not have a meeting place in Donhead and members go to Shaftesbury. They do have a burial ground set aside for them at Chilvercombe Bottom, Ashgrove. They can maintain their right to the land by decennial visitation.

Principal Houses and their Families

O NE OF DONHEAD'S most attractive features is the large amount of woodland and hedges. Nowadays we talk much about conservation and the environment but old photographs of over a hundred years ago show very few trees and hedges. People used and relied on wood in all aspects of their daily lives. They heated their homes with firewood, hedges were laid and the wood taken out was used for fencing, Faggots were made on which to build corn ricks to keep them dry: buildings and fences were made using local wood and the basket makers and hurdle makers used all the suitable materials they could get their hands on. Ashmore hurdles were always the best as the wood took longer to grow on the chalk soil and, therefore, lasted longer.

In the eighteenth and nineteenth centuries there were several large estates in Donhead such as Wardour, Ferne, Wincombe, Charlton and Coombe. The owners of each of these put tremendous resources into creating gardens and parkland – each wanted to go one better than his neighbour! Today Donhead benefits from the planting of these well planned and carefully designed parklands, including deer parks. Some of them imported trees considered very exotic.

Much of the wealth that enabled the creation of these parklands came from trade in an expanding British Empire, although it came at a tremendous cost in human life, wars and mutinies. But the owners of these estates were among the ruling classes and they had to keep up their positions for they felt set apart from the ordinary people. Too often, while maintaining an extravagant lifestyle for themselves, they did not pay those under them enough in wages and kept them poor. This was their eventual ruin and by the end of the nineteenth century many of them faced financial problems. After the two wars many of them sold to different groups of people, such as industrialists, financiers, lawyers and housing developers.

Many of the big houses in Donhead were built at about the same time and of the local greensand stone. They are broadly similar in their architecture and their distinguishing features are mostly due to their sites and aspects and to the views they command.

Charlton House in 2000.

Charlton House was built about 1821 (enlarged from a smaller cottage) and was named Charlton House between 1848 and 1855. It became the principal home of Robert Graves, whose family came down from London, and he quickly built up a large estate in Charlton. Throughout Charlton village there are still many small houses with similar architecture and Charlton House itself is very similar in design to Wincombe House.

At that time wide ranging technological advances which led to the Industrial Revolution led also to the Agricultural Revolution. Many new methods of cultivation and practice were put into effect and the Graves built Manor Farm in Charlton as a Model Farm, to try out all these new ideas.

The Charlton Estates were sold in portions in 1913. Charlton House was sold to Baroness Wynford and her daughter Gertrude Best. Captain Brocklebank then bought it in 1950 and Richard Hedges bought the house in

1958. He also bought Charlton Middle Farm and Holly Bush Farm. Most of the Charlton Estate, including Manor Farm, was bought by S. J. Blanchard who left it to his son Roy and it then passed to his grandson J. S. Blanchard.

Coombe House (now St Mary's School) stands on a spur between two wooded valleys with a lake and fishponds below. There is a spring below at Nunswell where Coombe House gets its water even today. Perhaps the nuns from Shaftesbury Abbey used to collect water from the Coombe well: it is not too far. The house was built in 1886 by Mark Beaufoy, a vinegar manufacturer. He was the MP for the area and quickly built up a large estate of 243 hectares through the Coombes, including Knight's Barn Farm and land along Salisbury Road. There are at least two farmhouses in the Coombes with his coat of arms over their doors.

The south wing of the house was enlarged in 1911 as a ballroom, to celebrate the marriage of his daughter. His son sold Coombe House and all the land, except for 50 acres (20 hectares), in 1930. It became Coombe House Hotel from 1931 to 1935 but was never really successful in such difficult times. During the second world war the American Red Cross used it for convalescent soldiers.

Donhead Hall in 2000.

Former Back Drive lodge to Donhead Hall on the old drove road (now Clover Hill) in 2000.

In 1945 the sisters of the Institute of the Blessed Virgin Mary (IBVM) bought Coombe House (rats and all, according to a private video!), with 145 acres (18 hectares) of land, and opened St Mary's Convent School for boarding and day girls.

Donhead Hall belonged to Reynaldo Weekes in 1658 and his widow gave it to his nephew, Luke Weekes, owner of Wincombe Park. His daughter, Mary, married Godfrey Huckle (d 1781) who changed his name to Kneller in 1731. It then passed through three generations of the family until it was sold to Charles Wyndham in 1825. He enlarged the estate with land bought from Baron Arundell and then sold it to John du Boulay, who died in 1895. His executors sold an estate of 214 (87 hectares) acres in 1896 to H.R. Blackburn and Captain H.C. R. Brocklebank bought it in 1943. When he moved to Charlton House in 1950, Mrs V. Tennant, grandmother of Richard Arundell, purchased the Hall.

Mrs Tennant sold to Mr Horne in 1957 and the family lived there until 1991. It was then purchased by Charles McVeigh who did much restoration before selling to Paul Brewer (2003) who has continued to restore the Hall to its former glory.

Donhead House was built in the late sixteenth century and, looking at it from the garden, part of the original Queen Anne house can still be seen on the right. It was the Rectory in 1704 and extended in the mid-eighteenth century. But, in 1892 the then Rector, the Revd. Horace Chapman, bought the house, resigned the living and became a Roman Catholic. The church authorities then had to build the New Rectory, Beauchamp House, which remained the rectory until 1939 when it was sold. The Rector of Donhead St Andrew, the Revd. E.J. Mitchell, then had to live in Greenways, Donhead St Mary, until a new rectory was built in West End Lane, Donhead St Andrew in 1955 for the Revd. John Godfrey.

It must have been quite an upheaval for the village when Horace Chapman became a Roman Catholic. He was 'a man of no small means' and was chosen to marry Agnes Pitt-Rivers to Walter Grove, in 1882. This was a

Donhead House in the 1970s.

large society wedding in St Peter's, Eaton Square in London. His own daughter married Viscount Allenby and another married Admiral Napier. The story goes that for his daughter's wedding a red carpet was laid from the front door of Donhead House to the west door of St Andrew's Church.

After buying Donhead House Horace Chapman enlarged it again. He built a walled garden, landscaped the park and field to the south-west, constructed two lakes above the house and included the river Nadder in the parkland design. Not content with all this Horace Chapman encouraged the Roman Catholics in the parish – estimated to be about 122, including children, in 1864 – to build a chapel on the top of the hill dedicated to St Bartholomew, in 1887. The chapel was served from Wardour and mass was said each Sunday until it was closed in 1960.

During the Second World War Donhead House was used by the Red Cross for convalescent soldiers and then it became the home of Sir Anthony Eden for a short time before he moved to Alvediston. It was then bought by Rank Hovis McDougall for a training college for licensees and for experimental farming. In 1990 it became the private home of Robert and Clare MacDonald.

Ferne is first mentioned in the Shaftesbury Abbey records in 1024, during the time of the Abbess Eulalia. In 1256 Philip de Ferne was granted a life estate and it remained in that family until 1450 when it passed to John Brockway through his wife Edith. The Brockway family held it until 1561 when the first

Ferne House in the 1920s.

William Grove bought it. (Robert Grove of Shaftesbury, first mentioned in 1498, signing documents for the Abbess was part of this family).

Ferne House was the home of the Grove family until 1902. The Grove family had a great influence over the area. In their early years they were administrators and rose to fame as reforming liberals and non-conformists. Two members of the family became MPs at Westminster, joining in the court and social life in London and in south Wiltshire and north Dorset. In its heyday 200 guests danced in the ballroom and had Fêtes on the lawn for 3,000 people. At the sale in 1900 the area of the estate was 2,000 acres (810 hectares), 800 sheep, 90 cattle and 15 horses were sold, along with the Grove Arms Inn in Ludwell and the Grove Arms in Berwick St John (now the Talbot). A very interesting account of the life there of the Groves family between 1809 and 1925 is to be found in *The Grove Diaries*, edited by Desmond Hawkins.

The Charlesworth family lived there from 1902 to 1914 when it was purchased by the Duke of Hamilton. Lady Hamilton lost her youngest daughter, Mairie, and became very well known for looking after stray cats and dogs during the second world

Wartime animals at a London station waiting to come to Ferne.

war. In 1964 the house was demolished as the Animal Sanctuary could not afford to keep it up. This was at least the third house on that site. Mr Newman Turner farmed there for a number of years and then Mr John Stancomb of Higher Berrycourt bought 185 acres (75 hectares) and the parkland was farmed by the Isgar family of Donhead St Andrew. Since about 2000 Lord and Lady Rothermere have built an interesting new mansion and have greatly improved the garden and parkland.

Leigh Court is the second oldest building in the Donheads after the churches, Wardour Castle and Lower Berrycourt. It belonged to Nicholas Leigh in 1412 and then passed to Sir John Leigh's daughter Anne, who married Sir James Worsley (1565). It then passed through several members of that family. In 1706 it was sold to the Revd. Gabriel Barnaby who sold it to William Brotherton, Sheriff of Berkshire, in 1758. He sold it to James Baron Arundell in 1819 with 123 hectares of land. In 1935 it was sold to J.C. Collett, with 101 hectares of land. Leigh Court has been owned by Michael Jodrell since 1952.

Over the centuries it has been greatly improved and modernised, with a large range of outbuildings when it was a 300 acre (120 hectares) farm. It commands a wonderful view over both Donheads.

The farm house of **Lower Berrycourt Farm** is probably the oldest building in Donhead apart from the two churches, Leigh Court coming a close second. It was the demesne farm house, built during the late twelfth century or early thirteenth century, with the parish boundary between St Mary and St Andrew going out of its way by half a mile to run

Lower Berrycourt Farm in the 1940s.

through the middle of the house. This was to enable the petty sessions for both parishes to be held in one room. There were two doors, one for each parish! This was also to accommodate the payment of tithes. In 1498 Thomas Grove lived at Berrycourt as an administrator to the Abbess of Shaftesbury. Although all the land in the district went to Sir Thomas Arundell after the dissolution of the monasteries (1539), the Groves continued to administer the district. They went to live at Ferne House in 1574. The Groves leased Berrycourt for three 99-year leases but put in a tenant. It was an interesting relationship between the two families during all the turbulent years of religious wars, for the Arundells were convinced Roman Catholic and the Groves staunchly Protestant.

With tenants living at Berrycourt the house has never had too much money spent on it to spoil it and take away its history. The smoke-blackened 'cruck' roof of an open hall survives today in the central north-east and south-west wing. The Groves may have lived at Berrycourt up to 1700 as they built on the new wing as a kitchen in 1669.

In 1795 the Arundells were selling off large areas of land in the parish to help pay for New Wardour Castle and they sold 300 acres (121 hectares) of Lower Berrycourt Farm up by Ferne House to the Groves, to become Higher Berrycourt Farm. More of Wardour Estate had to be sold off in 1946, when Lower Berrycourt was bought by Ralph Coward, the sitting tenant. In 1967 his son, Michael, took over the running of the farm.

A building on the site of **Shute House** was situated on the pilgrim route, which possibly continued to use the course of the Roman road for several centuries after the Roman occupation ceased. The building on the north side is thought to have been a hospital for sick pilgrims. It was later enlarged and became the rectory for Donhead St Mary. In 1291 the living was one of the most valuable in the Chalke Deanery, assessed at £13.6sh.8d rising steadily to £928 in 1831, making it one of the richest in the diocese. A rectory house existed in 1298 and was probably that part of the building at right angles to the road. The Revd. Rice Adams (1689-1737) built the south-west cross wing, containing two large rooms and a spacious stair hall. It remained a rectory until 1955 when it was sold, to become a private house and was renamed Shute House.

The Shute, after which the house is now named, is a spring of clear water which appears in the grounds of Spring Cottage. This water can only come from North Down which is part of the westerly rim of the Donhead saucer. It is undoubtedly one of the reasons why there is a large cluster of houses at the central hamlet of Donhead St Mary and why people congregated to this spot many centuries ago. This spring was vitally important to the village as its main source of pure water and in living memory people would go there to draw their water. It flows into the garden of Shute House and emerges under the wall bordering the road. After a few yards it crosses under the road and flows through the grounds of Shute House Farm down to join the stream at the bottom of Berrywood Lane and thence to the Nadder. In the grounds of Shute

Shute House in the 1920s.

House part has been diverted to created a formal pool with a water garden, eventually flowing south-west through Pond Close (formerly glebe land) where several artificial lakes have been created. The gardens were landscaped by Jeffery Jellicoe.

In 1086 Wilton held **Wardour** for the Abbey. The estate was later called Castle Manor of Wardour. After the dissolution of the monasteries the overlordship was acquired by William Herbert, Lord Pembroke, in 1551. The ownership, however, seems to have belonged to the family of Lord Lovel, who built the castle in 1393. In 1461 the land was forfeited from the Lovel family for supporting Henry Vl. The succession seems to have passed to and fro between the Crown and certain families, until 1541 when the Grevilles sold it to Sir Thomas Arundell, who already owned Tisbury, Hazeldon and Bridzor, in 1547. Between then and 1645 the fortunes of Wardour see-sawed. During the Civil War Cromwell's soldiers occupied the castle and in trying to regain it the owner succeeded in blowing up part of the castle, leaving the ruins we see today.

From the time of the building of Old Wardour Castle the parkland has been enlarged, making five ponds from a tributary of the river Nadder. Another pond, west of the Castle, has the parish boundary between Donhead St Andrew and Tisbury passing through it. It was greatly enlarged again at the beginning of the seventeenth century to make two deer parks, one for red deer and another for fallow deer. One of these parks was to the east of the castle and is now part of Horwood Farm, with the boundary marked Park Pale on our modern maps. This is where the Barons Arundell would have approached the Castle from Salisbury, coming off the coach road diagonally down across the downs to our present Shave Lane, by the polo field, and then across the A30 to Wardour.

When the third Lord Arundell died in 1694 the Arundells went to live in Breamore in Hampshire for nearly a hundred years, out of the way of public life and to live a quieter life financially. The fifth, sixth and seventh Lords continued to marry well. The seventh Lord married Mary, the daughter of Richard Belling Arundell of Lanharne, (from where they originated) thus reuniting two branches of the family. It was their son, Henry, who built the present castle **New Wardour,** 1770-76, considered one of the best in the country at the time. But, like all buildings, it cost more than expected and they had to sell a good deal of land to pay their expenses.

The fifteenth Lord Arundell had died in 1939 and the sixteenth, Lord John, died of tuberculosis while a prisoner during the second world war. The estate, therefore, had two lots of death duties to pay and had to sell many of their farms and cottages in the Donheads, except for a few around Wardour itself. It was a sad day for Wardour. The family still farms the remaining area.

Wincombe House is in the west of the parish. In the middle ages, land in the north and west of the parish belonged to Shaftesbury Abbey, and not to Donhead. It was known as Abbey Barton and an area of pasture as Heath. It was granted to Thomas Arundell in 1545 and William Herbert in 1552. Before 1688 it was owned by Luke Weekes and in 1754 by William Benson who sold it in portions, some to Godfrey Kneller whose son sold to John Gordon in 1808. It was the Gordon family who built up the Wincombe Park Estate and the house itself, in 1825. They were also benefactors of Donhead St Mary Church and there is a memorial tablet to Maria Gordon in the church. Mrs Hastings was the last of the Gordon family when they sold to Sir Arthur Bryant, the well-known historian, in 1956. The Hon. Martin Fortescue purchased the estate in 1962 and he has been succeeded by his son, John.

Public Houses

THE AMOUNT OF TRAFFIC carried by the A30 is illustrated by the existence in the early nineteenth century of five public houses in less than three kilometres. This traffic was in the form of wagons, traps, carriages and coaches and the high speed mail coaches, each wanting stops for refreshment or overnight stays. All these pubs would have had stabling for horses and accommodation for the night. The hardworking locals also wanted their drinks, social exchange and relaxation in the evenings. The population was larger and more locally orientated in the late eighteenth and early nineteenth centuries. Each pub served the area within which it was built and quite a bit of business was generated as the locals would not want too far to walk home at night! With three more inns in the Donheads – the Royal Oak, the Carpenter's Arms in St Mary's and the New Inn (now the Forester) in St Andrew's – there was no need to go thirsty – except in Ashmore which had no pub.

Arundell Farm was originally called the **Glove Inn** and has been a place of much history. In 1773, Stage Coach horses were stabled and changed there before climbing the hill. A Friendly Society with 114 members met there in 1803, but it was burnt down in 1810. It must have been rebuilt quite quickly as in 1812 the Groves from Ferne House would come for Boxing Day Balls each year to meet with neighbours. A Victorian Society also met there in 1839. It was then called the Arundell Arms. Petty Sessions were held monthly in 1848, but it was closed as an inn in 1906. Since then it has been the farm house of Arundell Farm bought by the Jeffreys at Wardour Sale in 1946.

The **Castle Inn** at Brookwater, which is just in Donhead St Andrew, was built during the early nineteenth century at the bottom of the two Brook Hills. It is sited by the bridge over the Ferne Brook and where the road from Rowberry to Brookwater and Milkwell crosses the A30. That bridge was mentioned many times in parish records as to which parish was responsible for the cost of

Castle Inn in the early 1900s.

repairs as it is so near the boundary. In the early twentieth century the publican, an ex-policeman P.C. Picket, used to keep his goats and hens at the back. After he retired the Ingram family took over as licensees, moving from the Carpenters Arms. When they left, in 1965, the pub became a private house. The restaurant called Bilbo's is almost opposite.

The **Lamb Inn** was built at the cross roads in Birdbush, between Win Green and Donhead St Mary but is now closed. 'Knocker' Case was one of the last licensees of the Lamb before it became a private house.

The **Grove Arms** at the bottom of Ludwell is probably the oldest building in Ludwell although it was badly damaged by fire in 1998. It was called the Talbot or Black Talbot from 1579 to 1811, changed to the Black Dog after 1811 and renamed the Grove Arms from 1880 to 1885. A Friendly Society met there with 50 members in 1803 and another Friendly Society called the Hope Society met there in 1830 but had ceased before 1906.

Grove Arms, early 1900s.

Grove Arms after the fire in 1998.

At the top of Ludwell Hollow is the **Rising Sun**, built in 1773 and called a beer shop in 1840. Francis Cox was a very well known licensee of the Rising Sun from the 1950s to 1970s.

Away from the main road there were three other inns. In Donhead St Andrew was the **New Inn** which changed its name to **The Forester** when it became a restaurant in the early 1980s. It has had many excellent chefs since then and serves a wide area in and around the Donheads, being the only pub in the central part of St Andrew. At the turn of the twentieth century it added a dining room / hall – a useful extension as there is no longer a village hall in St Andrew's.

New Inn in the 1930s.

Two pubs in the central area of St Mary which are now closed must be mentioned. **The Royal Oak** was a comparatively new building and existed to serve the area below the church. One of the licensees, Mr Shilton, used to keep sows in his garden at the back. The high bank has gradually been levelled off after it was sold as a private house. In the former garden a bungalow was built, called Acorns. It has now grown quite big – as acorns do!

Bar panels and seats were still in situ at the Royal Oak in 2000.

Finally, the **Carpenters Arms**, tucked away on the road to Semley, was the first pub to close after the Glove Inn. It was a strange site for a pub, with steep steps up to it and beyond and relatively few houses nearby. The Wincombe valley may have been a well populated area in the eighteenth and early nineteenth centuries and the Carpenters Arms would have been a good place for the

The Royal Oak in 2000.

locals. The Ingram family, who later moved to the Castle Inn, were the licensees. The pub closed in 1955.

The Carpenters Arms in 2000.

Schools

THROUGHOUT HISTORY the Church and other religious institutions have been responsible for education and for starting schools, hospitals and homes for the poor and elderly. The first school in **Donhead St Mary** was opened by the church in 1830 with two teachers, one the Parish Clerk and the other a dissenting minister. A school was built north-west of St Mary's Church by 1840 for 22 children. It was a red brick structure with a thatched roof, later used as a library and now part of a private house ('The Old Library') . In 1871 it became a National School but in 1875 the building was too small and was replaced by a new building – the present Village Hall.

Ludwell School, class 1 in 1930.

Ludwell School in 2000.

In 1842 a National School was held in the Old Remembrance Hall in **Ludwell** where a schoolmaster had 50-60 older children, mainly boys. In 1858 a dissenter helped by two women taught 12 older tradesmen's children and 25 younger ones at the Congregational Chapel, Birdbush. After the 1914-1918 war the school at Donhead St Mary was closed and pupils went to Ludwell School. This had two rooms and two teachers. Its numbers have fluctuated over the years. In 2003 the first schools reverted to being primary schools and now keep children up to 11 years old. To accommodate the increase in numbers a new classroom and school hall were built in 2003. It continues to serve the

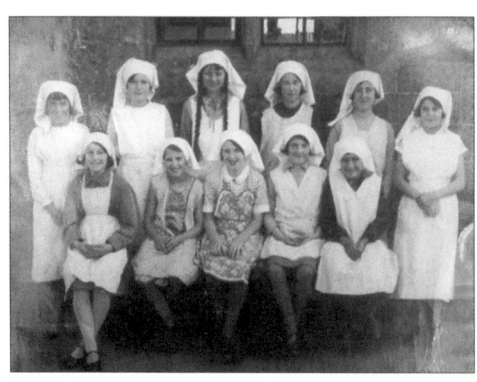

Cookery class in the 1930s.

Mr Dunning's class, 1950s.

Class in 1921.

Ludwell School, 1960s/1970s.

community and has been installed with all the latest technology. After-school activities include rugby football and gardening.There are now three teachers.

1906	-	114	1914	-	133
1938	-	73	1985	-	45
2007	-	61			

In 1945 The Roman Catholic sisters of the Institute of the Blessed Virgin Mary opened **St Mary's Convent**, a girls' private school, at Coombe House which now has about 350 girls. Originally the girls were taught by the sisters, but the school is now run entirely by lay teachers as the nuns were withdrawn for other duties. The buildings have been enlarged to make room for all the activities of the school. They have built a very fine school chapel. On the east wall is a mural showing the ruins of the old Shaftesbury Abbey after the dissolution of the monasteries. The artist is trying to re-establish the links with the Abbey and give the feeling that they have inherited some of its traditions.

St Andrew's School, just behind the church, was first held in the churchyard and later in the building to the north-east. It was built in 1835 with the income from the Revd. Bowles's Charity and started by the Revd. William Dansey. In 1910 there were 120 children but by 1938 numbers had declined to 58. The school was closed in 1970 but many of the children from both St Andrews and also St Mary's now go to Semley School. The building was bought in 1977 by the Henrietta Barnett School for Girls in Hampstead, North London, as a rural studies centre. The village is still able to use the building as a hall, with permission from the owners. Occasional social events are held there.

Mrs Bessie Sanger was a teacher in Donhead St Mary for many years. She is pictured in 2000 (top left) and with her husband Tom at their wedding in 1944 (bottom right). They lived at Minerva, North Down (top right), which has now been replaced by the modern house (bottom left)

The 20th and 21st Centuries

T HE START of the twentieth century saw England and the British Empire at the height of their power and influence. Donhead undoubtedly joined in the general zest for living as the rest of the country did. The large estates were, however, selling up because cheap food was coming in from abroad and farmers were unable to pay high enough rents to the landlords. Many smaller farmers were, nevertheless, able to become owner occupiers of the land on which they lived.

At that time there were many small craftsmen working in every village. These included harness makers, wheelwrights, blacksmiths, builders, engineers, carpenters and hurdle and fence makers. Community services were supplied by brewers and publicans, shop keepers, market gardeners, and hauliers. People providing personal services included butchers, drapers, shoemakers and tailors. Bread and milk and often vegetables and fruit, were delivered to people's homes. Older residents of Donhead can remember when nearly all of these services existed here. In the first half of the twentieth century transport began to change from horse and cart to the motor car, and garages came into being. The railway had come through to Semley and Tisbury and beyond, which meant that after goods had been hauled to the stations, first by horse and then by lorry, they could be sent on to London and elsewhere. Watercress, for example was sent from Donhead to Covent Garden.

Much of the local industry mentioned above had to stop when the First World War broke out and took so many men out of the villages. Many never returned – nor did the way of life they had left behind. Cheap food from abroad came in again and during the depression of the 1920s and 1930s large numbers of people were unemployed. Cheap manufactured goods also came into the villages from the industrial towns: local craftsmen could not compete. The social unity of the village and the self-sufficiency which had lasted for so many centuries began to break down.

The Second World War came to a country very ill prepared. It was a more mechanical war. (One Donhead man was making one Spitfire wing a day in a small factory in Salisbury!) Several Donhead houses such as Coombe House, Donhead House and Mansfield Farm were used as convalescent homes. Food production became vitally important because of the sea blockade, and agriculture was heavily subsidized. At the end of the war food remained rationed until the last controls were lifted in 1954 so agricultural subsidies were needed to keep up the nation's food producing capacity.

At this time there were still about 100 farms, big and small, in the Donheads, many families living off the returns from 15-20 cows, which had to be milked by hand into a pail. Mechanization came in at an ever-increasing pace – the little grey 'Fergie' tractor soon more than halved the number of carthorses working on the land. There was neither money nor manpower to keep the horses working, as a tractor could work ten times as fast. As new houses were needed the building industry got under way: many of the old ones were in a state of bad repair and needed modernizing. Builders were able to pay better wages than farmers and therefore took even more men off the land, which in turn necessitated more machinery.

It is important to stress how motor transport has completely changed the whole tempo of life. A carter had to be up at 5.0 a.m. to feed and prepare his horses, then back to breakfast by 6.0 a.m. to be ready to take the horses to work by 7.0 a.m. If the work required was ploughing it was possible to plough an acre (a Domesday book measurement) by 3.30 p.m. – horse and driver having both had a nosebag for lunch. Then it was back to the stable to settle the horses for the night and home by 5.0 p.m. in winter. It was a twelve hour day for two horses and one man to plough one acre.

With a heavy load it was necessary to avoid steep hills and it was sometimes necessary to go a long way round to seek an easier gradient. A trace horse could be put on for extra help. On steep hills a drug shoe could be put on to stop the wheel going round or a roller could be put behind the wheel to stop the cart from running backwards down the hill.

Glyn Barn in the 1970s (left), and in the 1990s (below). Several Donhead farm buildings have been converted for residential use during the last two decades.

But probably the greatest change to Donhead after the war was the Wardour Sale. The estate found itself with two lots of death duties to pay in 1946. This meant that the family put up for sale all their land and properties in the Donheads and went on selling until they had raised enough capital to pay off the tax. It is a great injustice of our system that although one may fight and die for one's country it taxes one's family hard.

This great sale meant that tenants became owner occupiers as many small cottages were purchased by the estate workers living in them. Large and small farms were bought by the tenants and some smaller farmers were able to buy land next to their own properties to increase the size of their holdings. This was quite an upheaval socially and financially but many people benefited. Wardour Estate, however, which had been so strong since the sixteenth century was now down to just a few farms in Wardour and St Andrew.

Another great change to Donhead came with the building of council houses in Overway and then a larger estate of about 50 houses around Charlton church and Ludwell School (Coronation Drive). The building of these two estates halted the decline in population in the Donheads and enabled local people to stay in the villages. They sold their cottages and moved to the council estates. The old houses were often in a bad state of repair but they were soon bought and modernised by retired people from outside the village. At the time a local thatcher remarked that it was a good thing that this outside money was coming in to repair the lovely old cottages as the locals couldn't afford to do them up.

It was probably in the 1950s when the first person living in Donhead caught a train at Tisbury at 7.0 a.m. for London, returning to Donhead in the evening, five days a week or sometimes just at the weekends, giving rise to the phrase 'They're weekenders'. This pattern has continued ever since: the cottages have been bought for weekend homes and when the children go to school the wife often stays down in the country all week. Frequently the little cottage is not big enough for a growing family and an extension is put on the end, sometimes followed by a second and even a third – the cottage soon becomes a large house. Of course, this does not apply only to Donhead but is a countrywide trend, for railway lines and motorways encourage growth along the corridors they serve. The telephone, fax and internet have helped this and it is now possible to do much work from home. Several businesses have grown up in the village, although building and gardening employ the largest numbers of workers. Many people move here because there are several good schools nearby.

All this has meant that the people who live in Donhead are not as dependent on the village as they were up to 75 years ago and the social life of the village is not 'self-contained'. TV amuses us rather than local pantomimes. We no longer depend on our neighbour as we once had to. Our extended families live outside the village and we frequently visit them or travel abroad. Farming has changed and the few farms that are left are managed and run by family members and contractors. It is interesting to note that several of the larger landowners, like their predecessors two or three centuries ago, are building up estates by buying many of the cottages and fields and using them for their employees or renting them out. Donhead at the beginning of the twenty first century is certainly very different from a hundred years ago. Our preoccupations are with traffic and the state of the roads not farming! People move in and out and in every aspect of life we are greatly influenced by national and international events and politics.

Tulip Tree, formerly Sunny Bank

Wincombe House

The Malthouse

Glyn Farm

New Remembrance Hall

Charlton House

Coronation Drive

Ludwell Stores

The Forester, formerly the New Inn

Grove Arms (renovated after the fire)

Buttling, The Butcher

Burltons

Shute Farm

The Old Stores, Donhead St Mary

Shute House

Donhead Hall

Ferne (painting by Tim Scott Bolton)

Donhead Memories

Bill Sansom

I WAS BORN in Lower Wincombe Lane, in the house opposite Lower Wincombe Farm. I was one of a pair of twins. When I was a year old, we moved to Laurel Cottage in Watery Lane, Donhead St Mary. There was no mains water in those days; like everyone else in the area, we scooped our water from a catch pit near the house. It came down between two hedges from the ponds in the Rectory gardens (now Shute House). Sometimes the cattle would get into the stream between the hedges and pollute the water . . . But lookl! Here I am today. It did us no harm!

We lived in Laurel Cottage until I was sixteen. Donhead St Mary had everything for us. The field behind the cottage was called Pond Close and belonged to Harry Wyatt who had the shop. He allowed the parish to use the field for recreation. The Revd. Courthorpe

Jack Sansom's forge near the old library, 1950s.

built a four-rink bowling green which was immaculate. There was a football pitch and we also played cricket. We had boating competitions on the ponds and used the Rectory gardens for scouting. I joined the church choir and enjoyed the choir outings to Bournemouth and other seaside places. At Christmas, we always had parties at the Rectory.

My grandfather, Jack Sansom, was the village blacksmith. His forge was near The Old Library. He probably made all the iron gates for the village as well as the gates for Donhead Hall and the railings around its deer park. He built

The Grove Arms, Ludwell in the early 1950s.

bicycles, too, and the first one he made he rode for six months to make sure it was alright. He was the first man around here to repair a pneumatic tyre. He broke up some cutlery to get the tyre off. So he worked out how to do it and then went round to all the cycle dealers on his penny-farthing to tell them about it.

Jack also cut hair and was the dentist. If you had a toothache and preferred not to walk to Shaftesbury to have it dealt with, you went to him. He would put a sackbag on the anvil and sit his patient on it. 'Which one is it?' he would ask and with his blacksmith's pliers would pull it out!

I got married in 1950, took over the Grove Arms with my wife, Joyce, and ran it

Sansom's Garage, almost opposite the Grove Arms, 1950s.

for twelve years. Then I bought my father and uncle out of their business (they were both mechanics) and built a garage on the site of Harringtons' Wagon

Works on the A30. This later became Birdbush Garage. In my day it was 'Sansom's Garage'. I was there for twenty years until I retired at 59 and came to live here.

Restored wagon made at Birdbush works, now in the possession of Randolph Hiscock, Coombe Corner Farm, Donhead St Andrew.

Doug Sanger

I WAS BORN in a little tied cottage farther up Watery Lane. Both my parents used to work at Donhead Hall. My father, Tom Sanger, had been married before and his son, also called Tom, went on to spend 22 years in the navy. After his first wife died, father married my mother, Emily Grace, in 1920. They had four children: Christopher who worked as a butcher and baker in Shaftesbury, my sister Eva, David who was a plumber and builder and myself, the youngest, in 1932.

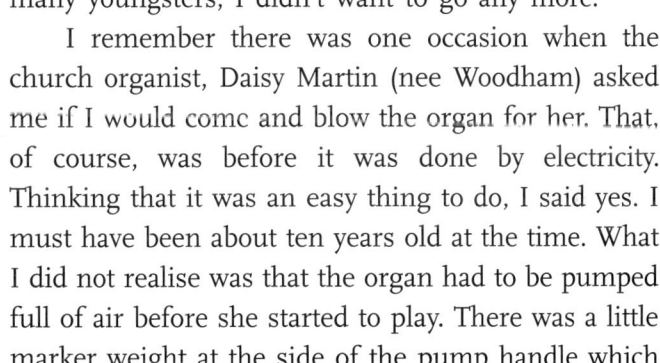

When I was young I went to Sunday School and the first teacher there I remember was Miss Emmy Dunston who used to live at Burltons. It was held opposite the village hall in a thatched cottage now called The Old Library. Later I went to the Sunday School in the Methodist chapel here at Donhead St Mary until I was thirteen when, like many youngsters, I didn't want to go any more.

Miss Emmy Dunston, with a Roman bowl found in her garden.

I remember there was one occasion when the church organist, Daisy Martin (nee Woodham) asked me if I would come and blow the organ for her. That, of course, was before it was done by electricity. Thinking that it was an easy thing to do, I said yes. I must have been about ten years old at the time. What I did not realise was that the organ had to be pumped full of air before she started to play. There was a little marker weight at the side of the pump handle which had to be at its highest point so as to allow her to play. I hadn't realised this and, when she started, there was just one note from the organ and nothing more. Someone else with more experience would have realised the weight had to be pumped right up to the top.

The Old Library, 1980s.

Needless to say, I was a bit embarrassed!

We used to have floods in Watery Lane when I was a boy. On those occasions we used to have to go up through Donhead Hall in order to get to school at Donhead St Andrew because the water was so deep. I haven't seen that for a good many years now, but there are many springs around here. One of the most powerful is at Shute House as well as those at Wincombe Lake. In our cottage it was very crowded until Chris went into the army. We had just two bedrooms shared by the girls and boys; there was no running water. You had to queue up for a wash and having a bath was a difficult business.

At Christmas time, all the children of the workers at Donhead Hall were given either a half a crown (2/6d old money) or a Christmas stocking, depending on the age of the child. It was always something we looked forward to. We also enjoyed the winter snow, descending the hills with our sledges or tin trays.

About 1949-50, the Donhead Cycle Speedway Team was first established and I was an enthusiastic member. Originally called the Donhead Daschunds, they later became the Donhead Dragons. The track was at Brook Hill to start with, but soon changed to the Remembrance Field at Charlton. Those were exciting times with hard-fought races against good local teams like Melbury

Donhead Dragons Cycle Speedway Team in the late 1960s.

Dragons have a reunion to mark the 65th birthday of Frank 'Buffer' Mead, 1994

Abbas, Heytesbury and Blandford. The Dragons consisted of eight riders and we kept ourselves solvent by organising dances and other social events. I was also a member of the army cadets, run by Mr Bill Penny, until I was called up to serve King and Country.

The change to the village we see today really began after the war. The motor car had a lot to do with it. When you had to walk or cycle you were much more in contact with people. The local community was your whole life. You married in the area and when you were children you all played together. The actual time of change is difficult to define. Most of the children lived in tied accommodation and when they got married, many moved to the new council houses. That is when the community started to change as most of the old tied cottages were sold to private buyers after the war when the Charlton council houses were built.

Fred Peckham

I WAS BORN at Hope Cottage, Donhead St Mary, at Jenkins Corner through the Wincombe Valley. Father was born the wrong side of the blankets! It's no disgrace today but was considered so then. He was brought here as a baby and left on the door step. Father's father was a widower when Reuben, my father, was born so it's not quite so bad!

Mother died when I was nine. Father, Reuben Peckham, was a market gardener. We went into Salisbury twice

High Bank, Church Hill, 2000.

Methodist Chapel, Donhead St Mary.

a week. When father was fourteen, his father started him going to Salisbury with a donkey and cart. When he had two donkeys he thought he was the Lord of the Manor! When I was six months old we moved to Churchill at Donhead St Mary by the church. It had been a bakery and shop but Eden Tanner, the previous resident, went bankrupt. We moved in with six children. We were never allowed to go out into the road to play. My earliest memories were of the chapel. Mother and father, Reuben and Meline, were Wesleyan Methodists at Donhead St Mary where she had lived at Watery Lane Farm.

We were never friends with father (children should be seen and not heard!) We were afraid of him until he was an old man and then he opened up more. Esther and I were the youngest. I remember my father dragging me to school. The roads were not tarmacked then and during very hard frost we had to have socks pulled over our shoes to keep them from slipping and I refused. Mrs Curnow was the teacher at that time. She wore a bonnet tied underneath and had long flowing skirts. Her daughter Eva was the second teacher. She also wore long skirts but had elasticated boots as well. When the weather was bad she used to hold up her skirts so they did not drag in the mud. George Scammel was a friend of mine. Another friend later showed him a photo of himself as a boy with his hand under the seat of his trousers. He confessed that this was because his trousers had holes in them.

I stayed at home after I left school. I had a horse then and was always happy with them. I helped run the family business: fruit, vegetables, eggs packed in baskets with straw. When we went to Salisbury Market, father did not go to bed but stayed up to prepare the wagon. Ernest, my brother, was a man when he was fourteen and going to Salisbury regularly as well as to Fovant Camp during the First World War to bring back pig swill (we found knives and forks and all sorts of things!) This had to be boiled so I had to get wood and get the copper going.

When I started to go to Salisbury Market, father had stopped going. He would still get up and get the horses ready. Ernest and I got up about two o' clock in the morning and had boiled eggs before we started. Father would have the wagon ready by the gate and would come with the trace horse as far as Overway. It was dusk before we got home again.

On the other days we worked on the small holding. There were two acres of paddock at Churchill, seven acres behind Hope Cottage and before 1900, father had the ground on the top of the hill there, part of the Wincombe Estate. I remember him telling me he had difficulty paying the rent as times were bad. I think he also had odd bits of land around the village.

In those days, it was all small holdings. The people below us at Churchill, for example, had three cows. Henry was a shoe repairer; his brother Herbie would have to go across the fields to Shaftesbury and get the leather. (It usually included a stop at the Royal Oak for a half pint of beer and a half of rum!) The Gold's farm at West End had mainly pigs which were all small. John Ridout had four or five cows at Brown's Bottom. His wife also made gloves. Esther and I went there on Saturdays to fetch the butter. All the industry has now gone. Among others, there was a wagon works, a brewery, owned by a Mr Lush, a basket maker and a blacksmith. It was a self-contained village; even the entertainment was homespun.

Distant view of the old Royal Oak in the late 1920s, before it burnt down and was replaced by the present building.

Frank Avery had a brother Bill at Barford. Frank lived at Donhead St Mary and drove the mail van. He picked up the mail at villages along the way and at Barford his brother took the mail on to Salisbury. Then Bill brought it back to Barford and Frank took it on to the Post Office at Brookwater. This was by horse, of course.

Gordon and Sheila Jolliffe

Gordon's Story

I WAS BORN at Stream Cottage, Ludwell, right opposite the Grove Arms. All these cottages were almshouses in those days. I was the youngest of four boys. We got our water from the adjoining river. My parents were Bob and May Jolliffe. Dad was a painter by trade. My older brother told me that Dad liked his beer. When I was born, a message was sent over to him at the inn and he said that he would come as soon as he'd finished his pint!

I spent a lot of time playing in the pub stables opposite. I was five when we moved to another cottage behind the village shop. We didn't have any water here either and got it from the baker's at the back of the village Post Office and shop (Bertie

The old workhouse and cottages, Ludwell, 2000.

Scammell's). The water came down through the bakehouse to a pump at the back. I had large pockets into which I put handfuls of currants from the sack in the bakehouse as I passed through!

Dad rode his bike to Shaftesbury every day for his work. He was a Salisbury chap originally. Mum's family were the Ingrams. They worked on one of the local farms. As a youngster, I was a member of the Dragons' Cycling Team and raced on Mr Isgar's fields above Brookwater. Later we went to a field next to the Village Hall. Robert Jeffrey was the son of John Jeffrey who founded the

Ludwell Post Office in the 1920s. The bakery was at the far end.

auctioneer's firm. Robert and his wife, Phyllis, were concerned about the lack of activities for young people and did a great deal to improve things. They were marvellous people. They started a youth club in the Donheads which included several of their own children. Before that we used to congregate on a big grassy triangle, a huge rockery belonging to Gething's Nursery opposite Lamb Cottage (previously the Lamb Inn).

Robert Jeffery, compere of youth club concert

I went to Ludwell School from the age of five to fourteen. The headmaster, Mr Dunning, was very good to me. We had our own farm there with allotments and chickens and did all the work as part of our education. Mr Dunning used to take all the produce to Shaftesbury to sell. We used to have to dig a trench out in the field behind the school. With Dave Hare I used to empty the bucket toilets once a week into this trench.

Sheila worked in the Silver Wand Cleaners in Shaftesbury, but I knew her before as we went to school together. When the new Council houses were built down Dennis Lane, we lived the other side of the fence from each other. Sheila had a gramophone with records. I remember we played 'Twelfth Street

Sheila Lucas, now Jolliffe, outside the Lamb Inn in the late 1950s.

Rag', a jazz piece which we both loved. At school I don't think she could stand the sight of me. At seventeen we got engaged when I was called up. We married when I came out of the army when we were both twenty.

Sheila's Story

WE ARE QUITE an unusual couple as we had two Ruby Weddings. The first was a big affair at the Natterjack Inn at Evercreech, owned by Gordon's cousin. It was a really lovely evening. A few days' later, I was talking

to my sister-in-law and found out we had had it a year too early so we had another one the following year!

My father's parents lived up Peckons Hill, Ludwell, on the left hand side of the steep hill that went up behind the shop. It was a little stone cottage and grandfather worked for Mr Tatchell the farmer as a shepherd. My father and his twin brother Jim were in the First World War. Jim later went to live and work in Bournemouth. Father was a stone mason and bricklayer in the Donheads but later joined his brother building Bournemouth. I don't know how he met mum. Her name was Annie Littlewood and she lived up the road until she was seven. She was the youngest of the family and was born at a little cottage at Pigtrough Lane, Donhead St Andrew. She only had one brother, Albert. When penny farthing bikes were in vogue, she remembered him riding one. It got faster and faster finishing up in a hedge! Her older sisters were in service, some of them in Wales. When Grandmother married again, mother went to live with her sisters until she was grown up. She then also went into service working at Stourton House near Stourhead. She was a parlour maid there. Then she went to Stourhead House to work for the Hoares. I remember being taken by her around the gardens and the church where she told me about the servants always having to sit at the back. Her mistress, Mrs Hoare, occasionally spent a day at Alfred's Tower. Mum used to give a prepared picnic to the boot boy who accompanied her always walking several places behind. I never understood why she adopted this lonely routine.

During the Second World War, I remember the dog fights that occasionally took place overhead. Occasionally, the German bombers would drop their remaining bombs on the chalk hillside on their way home. There used to be a search light at the top of Zig Zag Hill. The concrete base is still there. There were quite a few evacuees, too. It was difficult to find them accommodation as everywhere was already crowded. Father dug an Anderson shelter in the garden. My special friend was Greta Lane. Her father helped prepare the shelter and it was a lovely place to play with our prams but I don't think we used it more than twice for its real purpose. We rode our bicycles up to Handley Green once because a German plane had come down there and crowds came to see it. There were prisoners of war, mostly Italians, working in the village usually on the farms. [Gordon adds, 'Several stayed at Higher Berrycourt Farm. They had much more freedom than the German POWs. They could visit the village and do whatever they liked. I remember the preparations for D Day. There were masses of military vehicles with the tanks churning up the roads. They camped at night all around Tom Rossiter's field to prevent them being seen from the air. A whole stack of new telephone posts were demolished by tanks on one occasion. I remember a high explosive bomb exploding at Barkers Hill. A big oil bomb went off in the allotments gardens too. At the end of the war everyone marched along Devil's Track (now known as Ann's Path) carrying torches to a big bonfire on Wyn Green'.]

Tank going through Ludwell during World War II.

We moved to our present house in 1968. It had one plum tree and as it was in such a pickle, when people came to see it we would say, 'Well, at least it is ours', so that is why it is called OURS! We couldn't get a mortgage unless the wood worm had been eliminated, but we couldn't afford to do this. The owner, however, so wanted the cottage to go to village people that she offered to pay for it. The price of the house was £2,500 but her kind offer was refused as it would not lower the amount of the mortgage we needed. She therefore paid for the work to be done. This generous lady was Ellie Grine, quite a character.

Ellie was an Austrian Jew who came to the Donheads in the war because her family were being badly treated. She had literally lived off the land growing nasturtiums and stinging nettles to eat as a salad. She had made her own butter since she was a child and churned it in a container on her back whilst working in the fields. Much later, her mother joined her here. She also had three evacuees living with her during the war. She was certainly different, very serious, dressed in black and never spoke. As children, we rather unkindly thought she was grumpy. Eventually she moved to Australia.

The Lamb Inn, Ludwell in the 1960s.

Horace Mullins

M Y GRANDFATHER was the landlord of the Lamb Inn at Ludwell from the 1890s. His name was Robert Mullins and he died on 6 May 1906 having been kicked by a horse he was trying to tether. The inn belonged to Matthews the brewers from Gillingham and in those days his widow was not allowed to carry on the licence. The Lamb Inn was on the corner of the A30 where the road turns left to Blandford. My father, Robert, built a shop in 1919 as a butcher's shop just down the A30 from the Lamb and we lived in the house next door until 1945. All four of us children were born there.

My grandmother, after her husband was killed, opened a little shop near the Methodist Chapel. She married again to a soldier named Frank Galpin. My father built his shop just after coming home from the First World War. He said that Mr Fanner, the local builder, built it for him with no written agreement and no solicitor, for £200.

Father paid him back a week at a time. He had a good business there until his death in 1952.

Horace was born in this house, and later a butcher's shop was built in front.

After I left school I continued to work with father in the butcher's shop. I enjoyed the trade because I loved meeting people. Cecil Beaton, living at Ashcombe House (now the home of Madonna) with his mother used to visit the shop. From about 1930, when I was four, I used to go to the Dr Barnardo's fetes at Ferne, the home of the Duke and Duchess of Hamilton. They were lovely days. There

The butcher's shop in the 1940s.

were rides on Shetland ponies which I particularly enjoyed, but one year the saddle, a sort of basket chair on the back of the pony, swivelled round and I grazed my face as I fell to the ground. I was taken into Ferne House where I was treated personally by the Duchess. We also served meat to Mr Shepherd who was valet to the Duke.

Bess and I met in 1942. She had bought Shaston House in 1941 for around £900 having moved from Lancashire where she worked for Baldwins helping to make barrage balloons. She started a nursery for small children next to father's shop. Being rather old-fashioned, when he used to see Bess and her friend digging the garden, he said, 'You ought not to watch those girls doing the digging. Go and do it for them!' That was how we met. During the war, having finished her training at Norland's College in London, Bess opened her nursery for the children of the village at her home. It was for the children of parents who were in the forces or doing work of national importance.

Robert Mullins, grandfather of Horace.

John Blanchard

M Y FAMILY lived at Churchill House, Donhead St Mary. Our families go back to the 1800s. There are graves at Charlton and Donhead Churches. My grandfather came originally in 1806. He was a veterinary surgeon from Swindon. He lived at Churchill House, but later the family moved to Manor Farm at Charlton around 1911 and we have been here ever since. We own up to 800 acres of a farm previously part of the Ferne Estate, at that time owned by the Grove family. It was considered a large farm in those days.

I was born in Grove Hill House at the top of the Coombes. We moved here to Peckonshill Farm when I was about four. Peckonshill Farm came to us in 1932 when my father bought it to form part of the Manor Farm Estate. As a young boy I remember leading the horses and wagons to the fields; there were cart tracks in those days where there are now concrete roadways. We had about 21 or 22 labourers in 1942/3. We worked hard but things went with a swing. Now there is so much hassle. Haymaking was a village affair. A jar of cider used to help them on. Although now 85, I still lead an active life, but my grandsons are playing a prominent part now.

I was educated at Shaftesbury Grammar School as a resident, but came home at weekends. I started on the farm straight afterwards, a couple of years before the Second World War

Church Hill House from Church Gate in 2000.

Manor Farm, Charlton, 1912

and continued as it was a reserved occupation. We had German and Italian POWs from Port Regis Camp to help according to how much work there was. We gave them their meals and some 'baccy' money.

In my 85 years, the biggest change has probably been the introduction of modern machinery. The old binders and reapers gave us six foot cuts; you had to bag it up and drop it down from the combines. Now we have 16/18 foot cuts and 200 hp machines. Horse power was then the main transport. In the early part of the War we ordered two tractors and they both arrived within an hour of each other! In those days we had about ten horses. The carters used to come and get the horses out, clean and feed them, then go and have their breakfast. Later, we would see them going out to plough or sow. It was a marvellous sight, much better than the noisy tractors of today!

John Jeffrey

My uncle jack and his father started the auctioneer business in Sunny Bank, Donhead St Mary with his office opposite. Maureen Bone's father, Jack Edwards, was gardener there. I was born on the 3rd December 1927. When mother and father were first married they lived in

Windy Ridge, halfway along the road
to Birdbush. They later moved here,
to Arundell Farm along the A30,
where father was already farming. My
grandmother and my aunts moved
nearby to Wincombe. We went back
several generations in this area. The
farm was the Glove Inn until 1880.
We still have the old inn sign, used
internally, here on the wall. Father
bought the farm from the Wardour

Sunny Bank in the 1930s or 1940s.

Estate in 1946 when many of the properties around here changed hands.
Father and I went to the auction at Salisbury. We were there all day and father
wrote down the prices as they were sold. They seem ridiculously low today!

After I left school, I did military service and then joined the farm. We
probably had six or seven men working on the farm at that time, but it has
gradually dwindled until now when it's only my son, my daughter and myself
working here. Nowadays we have to depend on casual labour for peak periods
like harvest, lambing time and Spring planting. There are just over 700 acres to
manage now.

John Jeffery, auctioneers, 1930s

Arundell Farm, formerly Glove Inn, 2000.

We had to sell most of the cows in 2003 as we were losing money producing milk. Since then we have increased the number of breeding ewes – we have more sheep now than we used to have. We still have some cattle, but not a large number like we used to have. We also grow linseed, wheat and barley as before but with a bigger acreage and a bigger combine as we do all our own harvesting. We still cut around 20 acres with a binder, a machine you don't see much these days, so that we can use the straw for thatching. There is quite a reasonable demand for thatching straw; not many farmers are keen on cultivating it as there is so much labour involved.

During the war we had three land army girls and some German prisoners of war who were good workers. Latterly, they used to live in a couple of rooms down at the old building. One did the cooking for the others but at the end of hostilities they all went home again.

Template of inn sign

John Mullins

I WAS BORN in 1932. My parents were Ernest Arthur and Lilian Dorothy Mullins. They moved to Home Farm at Charlton after their marriage in 1924 and remained there until they died. My Dad's father, Charles Mullins, was a carter and he had a bust up with a farmer he worked for and swore he would never work for anyone again and he didn't! He started a carrier's business driving from Charlton to Poole every week taking two days for the return journey.

Home Farm, Charlton, 2000.

At fourteen, Dad was working with his father at Home Farm, Charlton. He married Lilian Brown from Eastleigh in 1924. Her father was killed in the First World War and her mother died in the 1918 flu epidemic when she was sixteen leaving her an orphan. I was born in Home Farm. My sister, Betty, was five years older than me. As a boy I loved to harness my dog to a little cart. We also had a donkey which threw me off regularly!

When the Second World War started, I was seven. In the previous year we had foot and mouth disease on the farm. I was then only six but I still remember vividly looking out of my bedroom window and seeing the cows burning up in the paddock. They reckon that my dad went grey over night. There were no tractors then and our horse, Major, pulled the cows clear. The dairy was on the opposite side of the road to the paddock and we weren't allowed to bring the cattle up to the road to be slaughtered. We had to have a lorry to bring them up to the trench which had been dug. Tons of coal were brought up to burn them and to feed the brazier at the front gate where a policeman stayed all the time. This went on until the farm was fully disinfected which wasn't easy. Even as a young child, I was devastated by this event.

I met Maureen Hindon, my wife, at a youth club run by the Jeffreys' at Ludwell. Her father was a lorry contractor who came down from Finchley in London to haul chalk from White Sheet Hill for the local farmers to counteract the acid soil of the land. When Maureen was seventeen they

Ernest Mullins in the early 1940s.

moved from London to Cemetery Lodge at
Wardour. Her father was able to live there rent
free in exchange for digging the graves by
lantern late at night. This was after his driving
commitments during the day which included
transporting the chalk.

Eventually Maureen and her family moved
to the Pentagon, the house next to New Wardour
Castle. There wasn't much electricity around
then, but at the big house they had this gigantic
generator which had been used to power
searchlights during the war. I loved to go with
Maureen's Dad to service it; he was a good

John and Maureen Mullins, 1955

mechanic. When he started it up, the whole building vibrated! It provided
electricity for the House, the chapel and the presbytery.

Looking back, there were many social events. When we started courting,
we used to have wonderful pantomimes in the village. My best friend, Alf
Jeanes, and I were the comics. I remember Fred Peckham was the grand vizier
one time; he had the right voice for it and Mary Peckham's brother John was

Village Pantomime, 1940s or 1950s

the genie. He was very good too. Miss Thomas used to direct them. She wrote the songs and the words. I remember Ralph Coward singing one of them which went like this:-

> Stand by the land and the land will stand by you.
> Serve her with toil and sweat
> Husbanding I must not forget
> They're partners too.
> They're partners too.

Everyone in Charlton worked in agriculture except the blacksmith and Fanners the builders. With few exceptions, this carried on after the war. Some then went to Chilmark RAF Ammunition Depot, but the rest remained in local industries. Today, our daughter is the only one farming.

Mary Peckham

MARY PECKHAM was born at South Elmsall in Yorkshire, 'near the coal' and she still sometimes feels a Yorkshire Lady. Then, after living three years in St Ives and going to school in Penzance, she arrived in the Donheads before the war. Her father, the Revd. Christopher Teasdale, was the minister at the Congregational Church in Birdbush, and she remembers someone coming up to pass a message to him in the pulpit once, and there and then he interrupted what he was saying and announced the start of the war. Chistopher Teasdale had learned plumbing as a trade earlier on. He was thus able to carry on with his plumbing during both world wars as well as being a parson.

Manse and Congregational Church, Birdbush, built 1871, and photographed here in the late 1970s.

Mary worked in the village shop in Donhead St Mary, now a house called The Old Stores, very near the church. It belonged to Fred Penny, an uncle of

The Old Stores, Donhead St Mary, 1960s

her husband Irvine, and was run by Esther Peckham, Irvine's aunt. One of her customers there was Bird Hine who lived in Shute Farm. He smelt very strongly of cattle and smoked Craven A cigarettes. He had a bristly moustache with a yellow flash in the middle, due to the nicotine, and with his bushy eyebrows meeting the cap pulled low over his hair he looked thoroughly thatched. He smoked over the milk pail and the ash would fall into the milk, but when tested at Semley his milk always kept best. He would cool his milk in the shute which was the source of water for many villagers and from where water was piped to some houses.

Mary was also a teacher and for a time lived in Churchill Cottage. She taught as a supply teacher in Donhead St Andrew's where the headmistress was Mrs Snelgar, a talented potter and water colourist. Later she taught full time in Berwick St John before the school there closed in the early 1960s. She also played the organ in both Donhead St Andrew and Berwick and organised the carol services there. To get to school she would cycle from Churchill cottage to Brookwater and catch the 29 bus from the Castle Inn (where Milkwell meets the A30) to Berwick. But when there was too much snow to go any other way, she walked to school along the lanes with the snow banked high above her head on each side.

Besides shop-keeping, teaching, organ-playing and caring for elderly relatives, Mary also accompanied Irvine with the produce from their market garden to Salisbury Market on Tuesdays and Saturdays. She remembers selling sprouts when the boards were frozen with ice. They

Castle Inn, Brookwater, early 1900s

would stop on the way to Salisbury to pick up rhubarb from old Mrs James at Arundell Farm and strawberries and potatoes at Barford. She and Irvine provided a sort of courier service. On the way back they would bring Mrs Pemberton and her voluminous luggage. She was a very big lady and needed help getting up on to the lorry. So Irvine would heave her up using his shoulder and with help of a vegetable box to stand on. She was known as 'Queenie', and when they reached her home, Mr Pemberton would call out 'Have you got the old Queen up there then?' Biddy Dunstan was another to get a lift home. She lived at Burltons and kept mice. The place was a bit run down then. To one side was a big wooden door with 'Mouse Farm' painted on the outside.

[With acknowledgements to the Donhead Digest]

Maureen Bone

I LOVE LIVING in the Donheads! The villages always used to be known as 'Lower Donhead' (St Andrew) and 'Higher Donhead' (St Mary). In those

days, to about the 1930s/40s, the villages had a more individual identity because you had separate rectors for the two churches. Revd. John Godfrey was the vicar at St Andrew's at that time and Revd. Peel was here in the old vicarage which is now called Shute House. My grandfather, Fred Edwards, came here much earlier with the Revd. Sergeant in 1911 having previously been his gardener at Stoke Abbot in Dorset. My grandmother, previously Elizabeth Timpson, had been nanny to their children. My grandparents had three children, George, then my father John and Maidie who came much later.

I was born at 'Vale View', Gutch Common. I remember Eby Stone, who lost both his legs at

Revd Harold Peel, Rector of Donhead St Mary, 1941-59

The Malt House, 1930s

Gallipoli, sitting in the entrance of his cottage with his leather apron wrapped around him mending shoes. We used to take the bucket to get water near his home at Foxbury Cottage. Irvine and Ernie Peckham employed dad in their market gardening business at that time and they would take their produce to Salisbury Market.

I was at Gutch Common until I was seven. We then moved to the Malt House which is the big house just before the Methodist Chapel at Donhead St Mary. It was once the brewery. Father worked there for John Jeffreys, the auctioneer. We had one of the two flats there. Dad used to chauffeur Mr Jeffreys who was the founder of the firm. His brother, Jim, was the father of John Jeffreys who now farms at Arundell Farm on the A30. In those days the family had their headquarters at Malt House living opposite at Sunny Bank where father also gardened for them. My sister and I really grew up here but I moved to Church Hill later when I married.

I remember that things seemed to move slower in those days. We were a small community. The bus, driven by Dick Bartlett, used to come twice a week (Salisbury to Shaftesbury). We had socials every Friday, country dancing in the old Remembrance Hall at Charlton and we enthusiastically supported the Donhead Dragons Cycling Speedway competitions. They wore a sort of uniform with dragons up the front and would peddle around the cinder track like fury! Their chief rivals were the Melbury Lions from Melbury Abbass. It was great fun!

My father was very proud of his motorcycle and side car which I loved to sit in. We used to go to the Carpenters Arms (now a private house). The Ingram family were there then. Margaret, Sylvie and Iris were their daughters and Iris, the youngest, was my special friend. Margaret still

The Carpenter's Arms, 1930s

lives here in the Donheads working as a hairdresser. My aunt Maidie was in service at Wincombe House. When she came home to visit, Dad would always take her back as it was so lonely on those old lanes and tracks.

Maureen Macey

I WAS BORN in 1931 in Shaftesbury. When I was two we moved to Ludwell and lived in a cottage known as Cades. When I lived there it had two bedrooms and two rooms downstairs. Because the cottage had no damp course, one of the bedrooms and one of the rooms downstairs had a lot of damp. There was no inside water, just a cold tap outside which was not drinkable. I remember going with my father to where the River Don rises to get drinking water. This place was called Springhead.

A few years later my brother and sister were born. At both births my mother was attended by Nurse Whitworth who rode a bicycle with a basket on the front. Later on she had a little green Morris car with a soft top.

I remember we had a black dog called Jack and a terrier called Trixie. One day Mum sent me to the butcher's shop next door with a note and some money inside. She told Jack to go with me. Apparently Jack would often wander into the butcher's on his own and he would be given a bone. But this day nothing was forthcoming so he helped himself to a joint of meat off the slab. Mum was horrified and Jack never went to the butcher's again. When I

Dewey & Wheeler, Butcher, 1952

was four, we moved into a council house at Birdbush. It had a bathroom! At first I was scared when you flushed the toilet but soon got used to it. There was no electricity, just oil lamps.

On Sundays I did what most children did then and went to Sunday School. I went to St John's at Charlton. I went with Miss May Gatehouse who

lived with her sister Maggie at
the bottom of Peckonshill in a
house called West View. The
Rector was Canon Courthope
who lived in the rectory at
Donhead St Mary (now Shute
House). We always went to
the fete he held there every
summer. He had a golden
spaniel dog that was able to do
tricks like 'Trust and Paid

St John's, Ludwell

For'. If you put a biscuit on his paw and said, 'Trust' he would leave it alone. If
you said, 'Paid for' he would eat it. Every Sunday his dog would lie outside the
church while the service was going on. If it was wet or cold he would stay just
inside the church outside the vestry.

*The Grove Arms, with barn and butcher's
shop.*

In the spring we would go to the
river at Springhead which is along a
lane opposite the Grove Arms. This
was where the cress beds were. We
would collect frogspawn, hoping to
keep it long enough for it to change
into tadpoles, then frogs. This rarely
happened as the cat always tipped the
jar over or so Dad said! We also caught
minnows and sticklebacks with our
string-handled jam jars. We could pick
snowdrops, violets, primroses,
bluebells and cowslips. Never would
we pull up the roots.

We liked it when the council men came to repair the road. The lorries
would bring the barrels of tar and gravel and put them along the side of the
road. We would run across them from one end to the other. It was great fun
watching them put the tar down, then the gravel. We would get very excited
waiting for the enormous steam roller to smooth it all down.

I remember walking home from school with my friend Pat. We were
talking about how my Dad had told us that he and Pat's dad used to string a
long piece of rope across the road in Ludwell Hollow and wait for the

policeman to come down on his bike. Then they would raise the rope and take his helmet off. You guessed it! We decided to try it. But we didn't have a long enough piece of rope so we tied two skipping ropes together and positioned ourselves either side of the hollow and waited. Down the hill came the policeman on his bike. We lifted the skipping ropes and did not take his helmet off. We had not lifted the ropes high enough and we took the policeman off his bike instead. Luckily he was not hurt. He gave us a severe telling off, then we had another one from our parents when we got home.

Michael Coward

MY PARENTS arrived to farm at Lower Berrycourt Farm in 1932. They came from Mere via Gore Farm at Ashmore and I was born here just before the Second World War. I went to school in this house too as my mother, Daphne, ran a PNEU (Parents' National Education Union) School for about 12 or 14 pupils from 1938 to 1955. There are many people still in the area who went through my mother's school.

My father, Ralph, was quite a character. He was a very self-sufficient person and always tried to make things he needed rather than buy them. I believe he was way ahead of his time in his attitude to the soil, the environment and the avoidance of chemicals. He became an organic farmer partly because he considered fertilizer too expensive, but then he became strongly committed to organic ways and was a founder member of The Soil Association in the 1930s.

During the Second World War, I remember oil lamps in the evening and blinds over the windows for 'the blackout'. There was no electricity, no telephone, no car. We went to church and to Mere in our pony and trap. For water we had to do 100 strokes on the hand pump to have a bath. Mrs Bartlett came to cook the meals for the school and do our washing in an old wood-heated copper that used to smoke like mad! The Nativity Play for the children of the Donheads, started in 1941 in Mother's school and has taken place every Christmas since then. It was written by my father moving out from the house to the stable, an old thatched one, in 1972.

Lower Berrycourt Farm, formerly part of the estates of Shaftesbury Abbey, serving as a court house for both Donheads

I mentioned earlier that my father was something of a character. When my family first moved to the Donheads, the Cowards were regarded as very strange people who were into healthy eating and would sit around an open wood fire eating raw carrots! All through the village there were scores of small farms with independent self-employed people making enough to live on from

When the house was built there would have been a fire in the centre, with a hole in the roof for smoke. This picture shows where beams have been joined in.

The main beam through the sitting room marks the parish boundary between the two Donhead parishes

The thatched stable where the nativity play is performed

just three or four churns of milk a day – that's 30 to 40 gallons. To give an idea of the cost of living between the wars, let me tell you about Dratty Litten who lived in Donhead St Andrew and whose family are still in the village. He would go to the Forester's (then the New Inn), with one shilling, [5p], in his pocket. He would buy some tobacco and they would give him a clay pipe to smoke it in. That would leave him enough change to buy sufficient beer to make it necessary to wheel him home in the dog cart. This shows how little it took to have a good evening out with your neighbours.

With the changing rhythm of work on the farm through the seasons of the year: spring sowing, harrowing and rolling, calving cows or lambing sheep, through silage-making, haymaking, harvesting and bringing the animals back into the buildings again for the winter; through the calendar of the church's year which, unsurprisingly, fits in with the cycle of farm life; and with my folk dancing and the folk traditions which also have their festivals to celebrate the changing scenes of life; combining all this with an organic approach to farming and the aspiration of keeping the land in good heart, I have built up a pattern of life and beliefs woven from all these strands which so naturally complement each other.

[with acknowledgement to the Donhead Digest]

Percy Hare

Y MOTHER'S PARENTS lived in Pigtrough Lane. When her mother
died she lived with her grandparents whom she always called Mum and
Dad. Her aunts and uncles became brothers and sisters.

One of the teachers in the later years of my schooling at Donhead St
Andrew was Mr Lovell. When I was about eleven, he retired and the teacher
from Berwick St John's School, Mrs Warman, came as headteacher. If it had not
been for her I would not have done so well; she was so strict, but a marvellous
teacher. My father was at Donhead St Mary's school although my mother went
to the same as me here. There were about 80 children there in my time. It
closed around 1970.

The Donhead House Estate

Lady Pender was the lady of the village and her tomb is just inside the
churchyard. I do not remember her husband, Sir James. Lady Pender always
gave a Christmas tree and did a lot of good in the village including building the

Donhead St Andrew School, closed 1970. It is now owned by the Henrietta Barnett School in
London for use as a study centre. It also serves as a village hall.

Institute building halfway up Pigtrough Lane. That was supposed to belong to the village. There was even a village hall committee but after the Second World War, it was sold to Col Herring Cooper. After his death, Col Forbes, his son-in-law, took it on. Their farm lay opposite. After a few years, he sold it with the farm to the Rank organisation, one of the companies concerned with animal feed. They had it for a number of years and eventually sold to the Brewers' Association for a catering training college for pub owners for about 25 years. The Institute is now Barkers Hill Cottage.

My father was a painter and decorator and I finished up having the same job simply because after leaving school at fourteen in 1934, there was no work. For awhile I got a job in Shaftesbury at Young's, the now-defunct ironmongers as an errand boy. I pedalled a bike around with five gallon drums of oil as so many country areas depended on paraffin for heating and light. There were no long term prospects as at eighteen I would prove too expensive to the firm who would have to pay a full stamp for me and so get a new fourteen year old boy.

The building trade was looking up a bit in 1937 so my father got me a job at Berwick St John with him. I started an apprenticeship as a painter and decorator and stayed with them until just after the war broke out. Then I left to work at Guys Marsh where they were building a military hospital. I worked there until mid-1940 when the work finished. At the age of twenty, I joined up. Being motor cycle mad, I joined the Royal Corps of Signals as a despatch rider and reported to Reading which seemed the other side of the earth to me!

Percy Maidment

I WAS BORN and brought up at Rose Cottage, Watery Lane, Donhead St Mary in 1918 at the end of the First World War. There were twelve of us children living there. We all went to Donhead St Mary school at four years of age for two years (it is now the Village Hall) and then on to Charlton School for the rest of our education. We walked about six miles every day. Mr Dunning was the headmaster at that time, very strict he was too! I now have one brother in Kent, and one at Shaftesbury; that's all that's left. I was about seventh in the pecking order.

Donhead St Mary School, closed in the early
1920s and became the village hall

Ludwell School

My father, James Maidment, worked at Donhead Hall for 48 years and we lived at one of the cottages belonging to the owner, Squire Blackburn. He was a gentleman and played the organ at Semley Church. When we were little we had to touch our hat to him.

My father had two gardeners under him. There is a deer park at Donhead Hall and occasionally father had to shoot one for the house. He had several big glass houses including one for grapes and one for flowers. They used to keep one man at the Hall just to tend the lawns and other odd jobs. As a child, I used to help at the weekend, watering the plants and brushing up the leaves. Father died in 1963 aged 92.

Before Bill Sansom built his garage next door (now Will McLean's mobility shop) it was a wagon building concern run by Harrington and Sons.

Donhead Hall, built in the early Georgian period on the land called Belnap ('beautiful hill')

They had a big engine like the Stephenson Rocket. A workman used to go down to the river opposite the Grove Arms every day to get water to drive the engine. This provided power for cutting the timber from the woods for building the wagons.

In 1994, Stephen Woodhams, a landscape gardener from London, went to Donhead Hall where all my father's green houses were falling down. He got in touch with Mr McVeigh, the owner, and with his permission re-constructed the greenhouses into an exhibit at the Chelsea Flower Show. It was called 'Mr Maidment's Secret Garden'! The garden was re-created down to the brambles and lichens and a section of the original greenhouses was used as a tribute to the skilled gardeners of the past. It was considered one of the most inspiring features of the Chelsea Show and received a gold medal. My nephew and I were taken up to London to stay in a posh hotel in order to see it.

Vi Head

I CAME to the Donheads in 1918 at the age of seventeen from Cholderton to work as a housemaid at Ferne House. I stayed for five years until I was married. There were four housemaids and before I left I was the second. The Duke of Hamilton died in 1940 and the Duchess in 1951. They had a large family. There were twenty servants in the house alone including four housemaids, four in the kitchen, four in the pantry, four in the laundry plus gardeners and others outside. I was known as 'the dust hunter'!

Ferne House, built in 1811 to replace an medieval building

We had regular visits from Lord Fisher who was a friend of the family and I remember having to light his fire at 4.30 am – there was no central heating – 4.30 am until after doing the beds at night were my hours. I finished the day about 9 pm. We had prayers every morning – the Duchess or one of the family took them. I went to church at Donhead St Andrew, but if the family went to church, it was to Berwick St John. We had the afternoons easier and I had half a day and every other Sunday off. Nevertheless, I was very happy there. My sister was there for 40 years from children's nurse to the Duchess's maid.

Lord Nigel, one of the sons, started a cricket club at Ferne, but during the War the estate became an animal sanctuary as well as a home for orphan evacuees looked after by a matron and nurses [These were from the Waifs and Strays' Society]

After five years, I left Ferne to marry Fred Head. I met Fred at a 'threepenny hop' at the Institute at Barkers Hill. I was 21. Before the First World War, Fred worked at the watercress beds at Ludwell and afterwards for Mr John Jeffrey's father at Arundell Farm. He then became a builder and worked as an 'oddman' in Ferne House until the Duchess died. He was born at Birdbush. His father died when he was six leaving his mother with nine children. She then married again.

I remember the 'Chocolate Bus' which came from Barkers Hill and went to Shaftesbury every day. Mr Lewis was the driver; his father was the chauffeur for Lady Pender. Then the Wilts and Dorset took over and Mr Lewis went to work for them. The bus also went to Tisbury in time to meet the nine o' clock train. There was a Post Office in the village and one at Brookwater. Now there is nothing except the Forester Inn. Today you have to go to Shaftesbury, Salisbury or Tisbury. In those days there were tradesmen including a baker and a grocer, who came around to you.

Joyce Johnson

MY FAMILY farmed at Gutch Common, a sort of hamlet between the Donheads and Semley, for generations. My father, Ebinezer (Eby) Stone was different. He wanted to work with horses so his family sent him away to Stourton House, Stourhead where he learnt to become a groom. When the First World War started, however, he volunteered for the 7th Gloucester Regiment and subsequently, in some of the fiercest fighting at Gallipoli, he lost both his legs.

Whilst hospitalised at Norwich, father met and fell in love with a children's nurse. They were later married and when he was well enough, they returned to stay with my great aunt Emily who was the landlady of the Benett Arms, Semley. Here he was fitted with artificial legs before returning to his old home at Gutch Common with his new bride. He showed great courage and determination after his return walking with the aid of a stick on his new limbs. After the War Dad had a 100% disability pension and became a 'snob', a boot and shoe repairer, supplementing his pension with our smallholding and running a carrier service to the station at Semley with the aid of our pony and trap.

Hill House, previously an abattoir, is now known as Foxbury Cottage. It lies opposite the ancient Tittle Path at Gutch Common along the road to Donhead St Mary. I was born there in 1924 and grew to love it although my mother, being a city woman, found it very hard to adjust. Once I lost my beloved cat, heavy with pregnancy. Several days later, still grieving, I looked up to see her walking along the thatch ridge of the cottage followed by five little kittens! In those early days, the village of Semley was 'gated' so that the cattle and other animals could be let out to roam freely over the common and the green strips along the lanes during the summer months. Mrs Williamson, the school head mistress, used to tether her goats and ponies there too. Farms were much smaller then, often little more than smallholdings with a few chickens, pigs and cattle.

There were common gates at the beginning of Benetts Lane, at the turning to Sedgehill and on the Semley Station hill as well as ours at the entrance to Donhead Lane. I loved to open it for motor cars and was often given a penny or halfpenny for my troubles. I would watch eagerly every afternoon for Fred Potter's wagon taking watercress to Semley Station. Mr Hardy came every Saturday evening with his horse and cart to sell fancy cakes at seven for sixpence. Milk would be delivered in a can by Ernest Coward on his bike each afternoon to fill mother's waiting jug. It was not until around 1936 that milk started arriving in bottles from Kirton Farm.

Although my mother found the days long, I was rarely bored or idle. I collected water from the well at the bottom of the Tittle Path leading up to Castle Rings. There were few visitors, admittedly, but 'gentlemen of the road' would pass by on the route from Tisbury Union to Shaftesbury Workhouse and always stopped to ask for water. I fed the hens and the pigs kept in a sty in the garden and combed our pony old Bob. During the summer holidays, children would arrive from London to stay with us and other families in the village. Most of our holidays were spent at Knipes Farm, the home of Mr Nutbeam and his two sisters. They allowed us to watch the milking which was done by hand, assist at the haymaking and ride on the hay wagon.

In those inter-war years, bread and groceries were delivered daily. There was a taxi service run by Capt Bapty; his was the only house with a telephone. Mrs Grocott and her son Alan who baked the bread, ran the stores at Semley.

Firewood we collected from Oyster Coppice, the wooded area which lay at the back of our house where I picked primroses and bluebells for my grandparents. I would run errands for the older people such as shopping at our local shop run by Mrs Batten, collected library books from the school and medicine from the surgery at Donhead St Mary.

An annual picnic took place on Hart Hill at Shaftesbury, always under the same tree, with cakes and tea preserved in a bottle. There was an annual walk to Tisbury with my mother and my brother George. We bought sweets along the way at the little shop at Wardour and returned by train to Semley Station where Dad would be waiting to take us home in the pony cart.

My school days at Semley were happy ones although the teachers, such as Mrs Guy and Miss Doggrell, were quite strict. They taught us folk dancing which was universally popular then. We visited festivals at Trowbridge and Devizes and won the shield several times. We also performed at church and village fetes wearing white dresses with green belts and the boys in white shirts and green ribbons. In my last year at the school, before leaving in 1938, aged fourteen, we were taken weekly by bus to a cookery class at Tisbury. Held in an annexe opposite the church, I disliked it intensely preferring the sewing and knitting under the kindly eye of our headmistress Mrs Pitman (née Pyart) who was a very good teacher indeed.

Nor was our physical health neglected. The district nurse came frequently, lining us up to inspect our nails and our hair for lice. The dentist arrived annually. We received a third of a pint of milk daily and an unpalatable spoonful of white cod liver oil. There were also nature walks up Benetts Lane which I particularly enjoyed. They were a sort of observation lesson to see what we could record when we got back.

On leaving school I was employed at the sub post office in Semley delivering telegrams and assisting generally. At that time it was in a small hut near where the recently closed shop was situated. Mrs Doris James was the sub postmistress having been previously at the head office at Shaftesbury before her marriage compelled her to be downgraded. I later worked for her brother at Motcombe before being transferred to the main Shaftesbury office in May

1940. The Second World War had now started so life on the counter was very hectic (but wonderful!). I used to cycle back and forward from Gutch Common in the blackout and remained there until my marriage in 1949.

Despite his disability, Dad carried on his cobbling business until failing health compelled his retirement. He died aged 62 in 1956 and was buried at Cann.

The Chocolate Bus in the late 1920s or early 1930s. Run by the Donhead Transport Company, it operated from Donhead St Andrew to Tisbury and Shaftesbury. It was bought out in 1936 by Wilts & Dorset Motor Services.

A Donhead Gallery

This aerial photograph (taken by Tim Jackson) of Donhead St Mary around the church, looking south-eastwards, shows long narrow fields which may preserve the sites of medieval crofts or smallholdings and their closes.

Birdbush Waggon Works (above) closed in the early 1930s and the site lay empty for some years. It was bought in 1962 by Bill Sansom, who built his new garage there (right). Examples of a waggon and two carts manufactured there are illustrated in the catalogue below.

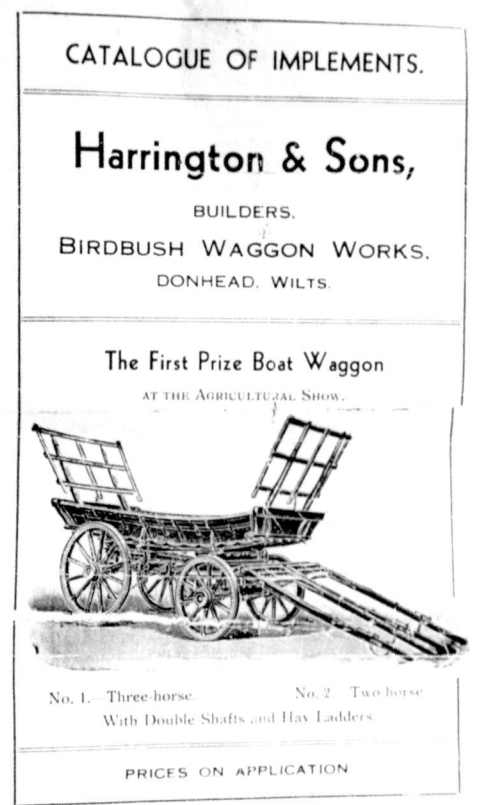

CATALOGUE OF IMPLEMENTS.

Harrington & Sons,

BUILDERS.

BIRDBUSH WAGGON WORKS.

DONHEAD, WILTS.

The First Prize Boat Waggon

AT THE AGRICULTURAL SHOW.

No. 1. Three-horse. No. 2. Two-horse
With Double Shafts and Hay Ladders.

PRICES ON APPLICATION

West of England Farm Cart

with 3½ in. or 4 in. Wheels, and Hay Ladders.

4-churn Crark Axle Milk Cart.

Two-horse Trolley

with Single or Double Shafts and Hay Ladders.

PRICES ON APPLICATION
Estimates for all descriptions of Carts, Vans, Waggons, etc., free.

Pearson & Son, Printers, Shaftesbury.

The old laundry, Donhead St Mary, is in the garden of a house now called Carpenters, but formerly a pub, the Carpenters' Arms. The big houses in the village sent their laundry here to be done.

West View, Ludwell in the early 1900s. The house behind (now demolished) was the premises of Gatehouse the tailor. In 1909 Gatehouse raised a football team (below) to respond to a challenge from another tailor in Shaftesbury. The story is told on the back of the postcard that the Shaftesbury team were so confident of winning that they offered to play for a silver cup, which they would provide. Later on the Donhead team discovered that in case their opponents lost they brought along a tin cup as well. In the event Donhead won 5-2, and the losers awarded them the tin one. Had Shaftesbury won they would have given themselves the silver cup

Hill House, Donhead St Andrew, around 1900, when it was occupied by the Jeffery family. Sarah Jeffery attended the county council itinerant butter-making school in 1895 and was awarded a certificate (below).

*William Henry Fry, who lived at Ashcombe Farm on the border of Donhead St Mary parish,
standing by the entrance to the Quaker burial ground in August 1930 (above left). The site is
tucked away deep in a valley between Win Green and the Tollard Royal to Shaftesbury road. The
Quakers make a pilgrimage there every ten years to uphold their right of way.*

*A view of cottages in Donhead St Andrew, probably taken in the 1950s. Sharp's Mill, now known
as Rickett's Mill, lies to the left of the picture.*

The Dewey brothers, Jim and Jack, blacksmiths at Donhead St Andrew, shown at work in the 1940s (above). By the 1960s Jack was also operating a haulage business from a depot in Mill Lane, Donhead St Andrew, where some of the fleet of lorries is parked, 1970s (opposite page).

View from the same point as the photograph on the opposite page, taken in 2000.

A view across Milkwell in the 1920s or 1930s.

This poor photograph (above left) shows a shop which stood next to Grove House in Ludwell and sold tobacco and sweets. Leopold Taylor was the shopkeeper there from the mid-1930s and through the early 1940s. Although now a cottage (see opposite page) the sign for Lyons tea remains. The white post visible to the right of the shop belonged to a rope works next door. Rope was attached to this for winding, and the rope worker would wind from a point right down the road opposite the Grove Arms.

The same view of Milkwell as seen opposite, but in 2000. Notice how the trees have now regenerated after heavy cropping for fuel and commercial purposes earlier in the century.

A recent picture of the shop, now a private residence, shown opposite.

Donhead St Andrew Post Office and Stores, a commercial photograph produced in the 1960s. It was closed during the 1980s. It was owned by 'Granny' Sharp, and is now called Corner Cottage.

Hare Cottage, Lower Wincombe Lane, in the early 1900s.

Members of the Hare family, who lived at their cottage in Lower Wincombe for several decades.

By the end of the 20th century, like so many other agricultural workers' homes, the original Hare Cottage (seen here in 2000) had been replaced by something on a grander scale.

A cottage at Ludwell in the 1920s (left) and in 2000 (right).

'Butlers', Lower Wincombe in 1949 (above), and in 2000 (opposite page, top). In recent years it has been the home of the inter-connected Chilton and Morris families.

Donhead St Mary from Lower Berrycourt in the 1930s. The Methodist Chapel is shown in the centre foreground. Bruins is prominent to the left and was constructed of stone from the old brewery. When it was built a Roman road was discovered beneath.

Donhead St Mary from West End in the 1930s. This view is fronted today by the West End council houses.

The Scammell sisters, Ella and Isobel, in the 1930s. Their father had the Ludwell Post Office Stores and a bakery next door. Both girls worked in the shop.

This family lived at Park Gate Cottages, part of the Donhead Hall estate. The taller young man in the picture left school at 11 to work as a dairyman at the Hall.

West End Farm in the early 1900s (above). It is shown (below right) with John and Helena Feltham in 2000.

*Tom Rossiter on his dairy farm at
Birdbush in 2000
(see page 17 for 40 years earlier).*

The former Brookwater Post Office, with
entrance bricked up (above); Mr and Mrs
Sid Mullins on their wedding day (left); and
on their golden wedding anniversary
(below). After 50 years Sid can still wear
the same suit.

Accident outside Brookwater Post Office and Telephone Exchange (on the A30 near the Castle Inn) on 25 August 1938. The postmaster, Mr Blandford, is sitting on the milk churn. The load of 17-gallon milk churns is being transferred to a second Nestlé lorry which is to be seen in the background.

Horace and Desmond Spinney working at Grove Farm, Lower Coombe, for the farmer, Peter Cooper, in the early 1970s.

Rev John Cox, rector 1970-1976 (above).

*Rev Tom Curry with Noel Mary Ward and Val Phillips, churchwarden and lay pastoral
assistant respectively (above right).*

*The New Remembrance Hall, opened in 1990 by Rosemary Blatchford, the daughter of John and
Helen Blanchard of Peckons Hill Farm.*

Christening with Rev Tom Curry, early 1980s, Donhead St Mary's Church (above); Group of parishioners outside the porch of St Andrew's Church, 1970s (below).

Donhead Cricket Club, 1950s.

Donhead Cricket Club v. Ladies International XI, August 1975, Tony Mitchell tossing coin.

Ladies International Cricket XI at Donhead, 1975.

Donhead Tennis Club, 1967.

Donhead Sports Club Committee, 1980s.

Donhead Football Club, 1972-73 Dorset League Division 4 North, Runners Up.

Donhead Sports Club, 2000.

Donhead Junior Football Team, 1980s.

Chapel School treat, Win Green, 1905.

Donhead Young Helpers League, date unknown.

The Taming of the Shrew, 1931.

Village Hall Pantomime.

Donhead Home Guard outside Ludwell School, 1940s. Seated in the front, centre, is their sergeant, William Penny.

Donhead Scout Group. The tall man in the centre is Mr Hastings from Wincombe Park.

Donhead St Mary Pageant, 1953.

Donhead St Mary Pageant, 1953.

Village Hall Pantomime, Cinderella, 1955.

Beating the bounds on Rogation Sunday, 1983.

Index

This is an index of people, places and selected subjects. References to the colour pages i-viii (between pages 64-5) are prefixed by 'col'.

A Sketch Map of the Parishes of ~ ~ ~ ~ ~ ~
Donhead St Andrew and Donhead St Mary
in the County of Wiltshire ~ ~ ~ ~ ~ ~ ~ ~ ~ ~

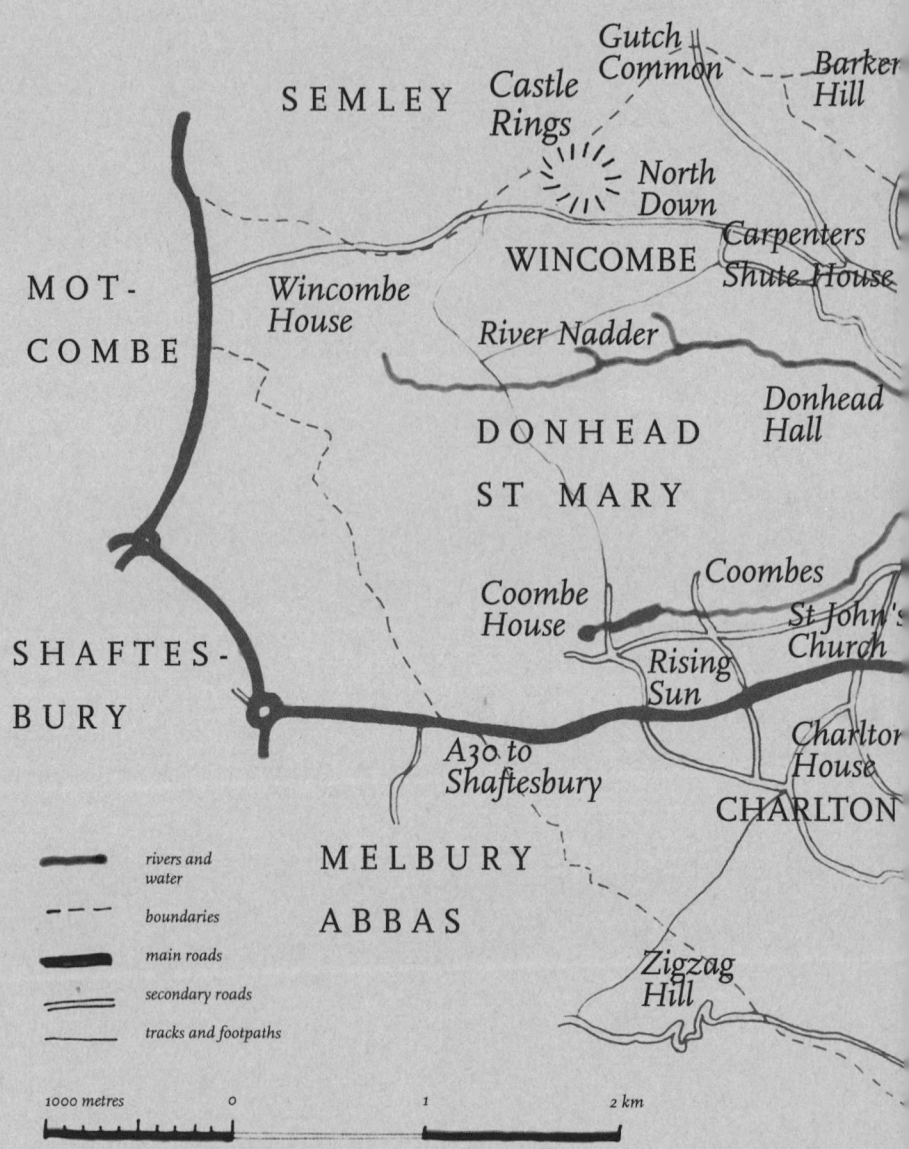

Gutch
Common

Barker
Hill

Castle
Rings

SEMLEY

North
Down

WINCOMBE

Carpenters
Shute House

MOT-
COMBE

Wincombe
House

River Nadder

DONHEAD
ST MARY

Donhead
Hall

Coombes

Coombe
House

St John's
Church

SHAFTES-
BURY

Rising
Sun

Charlton
House

A30 to
Shaftesbury

CHARLTON

rivers and
water

MELBURY

boundaries

ABBAS

main roads

Zigzag
Hill

secondary roads

tracks and footpaths

1000 metres   0   1   2 km